West Wales Railways

CARMARTHEN TO FISHGUARD HARBOUR

West Wales Railways

CARMARTHEN TO FISHGUARD HARBOUR

JOHN HODGE

Title page: Neyland County No. 1027 County of Stafford approaching its stop at Clynderwen at 3.24pm with the 2.40pm Neyland to Paddington in June 1962. The six coach portion would run through to Swansea where a dining portion would be added for its 5.30pm departure to Paddington. (M.J. Esau)

First published in Great Britain in 2021 by
Pen and Sword Transport
An imprint of
Pen & Sword Books Ltd
Yorkshire - Philadelphia

Copyright © John Hodge, 2021

ISBN 978 1 52679 578 6

The right of John Hodge to be identified as Author of this work has been asserted by him in accordance with the Copyright, Designs and Patents Act 1988.

A CIP catalogue record for this book is available from the British Library.

All rights reserved. No part of this book may be reproduced or transmitted in any form or by any means, electronic or mechanical including photocopying, recording or by any information storage and retrieval system, without permission from the Publisher in writing.

Typeset in Palatino 11/13 by SJmagic DESIGN SERVICES, India.

Printed and bound by Printworks Global Ltd, London/Hong Kong.

Pen & Sword Books Ltd incorporates the Imprints of Pen & Sword Books Archaeology, Atlas, Aviation, Battleground, Discovery, Family History, History, Maritime, Military, Naval, Politics, Railways, Select, Transport, True Crime, Fiction, Frontline Books, Leo Cooper, Praetorian Press, Seaforth Publishing, Wharncliffe and White Owl.

For a complete list of Pen & Sword titles please contact

PEN & SWORD BOOKS LIMITED
47 Church Street, Barnsley, South Yorkshire, S70 2AS, England
E-mail: enquiries@pen-and-sword.co.uk
Website: www.pen-and-sword.co.uk

or

PEN AND SWORD BOOKS
1950 Lawrence Rd, Havertown, PA 19083, USA
E-mail: Uspen-and-sword@casematepublishers.com
Website: www.penandswordbooks.com

CONTENTS

Dedication 6
Preface 6
Acknowledgements 6

INTRODUCTION 8
    Development of Fishguard Harbour 8
    West Wales Milk Traffic 15
    West Wales Fish Traffic 18

LOCATION ANALYSIS 20
    Carmarthen to Carmarthen Bridge 20
    Llanstephan Crossing 25
    Sarnau 28
    St. Clears 31
    Whitland 38
    Cardigan Junction 82
    Clynderwen 85
    Clarbeston Road 96
    Spittal Tunnel, Treffgarne, Wolfs Castle Halt 128
    Welsh Hook Halt 136
    Mathry Road 138
    Letterston Junction 141
    Jordanston Halt (Manorowen) 147
    Fishguard & Goodwick 152
    Fishguard (Goodwick) Mpd 168
    Fishguard Harbour 185

Appendix 212

DEDICATION

I dedicate this book to my late wife, Velda Margaret (nee Kirton), a native of Hayes, Middlesex. On leaving school in 1948, she became a shorthand-typist with the newly formed Western Region of British Railways at Paddington, in succession to the Great Western Railway, where she began work in the Rates department. She aspired to become a secretary to one of the officers and eventually to becoming a relief secretary whose duties included relieving the General Manager's secretary for annual leave, etc. One of her other duties was assisting the board member in charge of what remained of the Fishguard & Rosslare company's business during the 1950s, involving typing, book-keeping and general matters, thus having a link with the Fishguard element of this book. It was during this time that she worked with Eva MacDonald of Iver who also worked in the Rates department and who became a well-known historical romance novelist, an autographed copy of the whole of the 38 volumes of her works now residing in one of my bookcases.

PREFACE

I refer readers to my Swansea to Llanelly volume (published by Wild Swan Ltd.) in the series on the South Wales Main Line in which the Introduction gives a history of the development of rail services west of Swansea from the Victorian era through to the end of steam in the 1960s. I commend this to readers of this volume and ask them to study this as otherwise it would be necessary for me to repeat it in each succeeding volume. Carmarthen was dealt with in detail in the preceding volume, Llanelly West to Carmarthen, so this volume completes the section on the county town with some shots of trains leaving that location, and showing the famous river bridge over the Teifi and the railway beyond.

I also commend readers to the 1987 Wild Swan book *Edwardian Enterprise* by John Norris which contains a detailed account of the building and opening of Fishguard Harbour.

ACKNOWLEDGEMENTS

I am grateful to Pat Garland (whose collection is now held by Roger Carpenter), Alan Wild, Garth Tilt, Jeff Stone, Peter Jones and Mike Esau for steam age illustrations and to Stuart Warr for his modern colour photographs in various locations covered by this book. As usual, I have used the excellent layout details provided in the R.A. Cooke Layout series. I am also grateful to Tony Elliot, Richard Woodley and Richard Maund for their help with Irish and Trans-Atlantic boat services at Fishguard.

I have made every effort to identify all the copyright holders of pictorial and archive material used in this book. If I have wrongly attributed any material used, please email me at john_hodge@tiscali.co.uk if there is need to rectify the position.

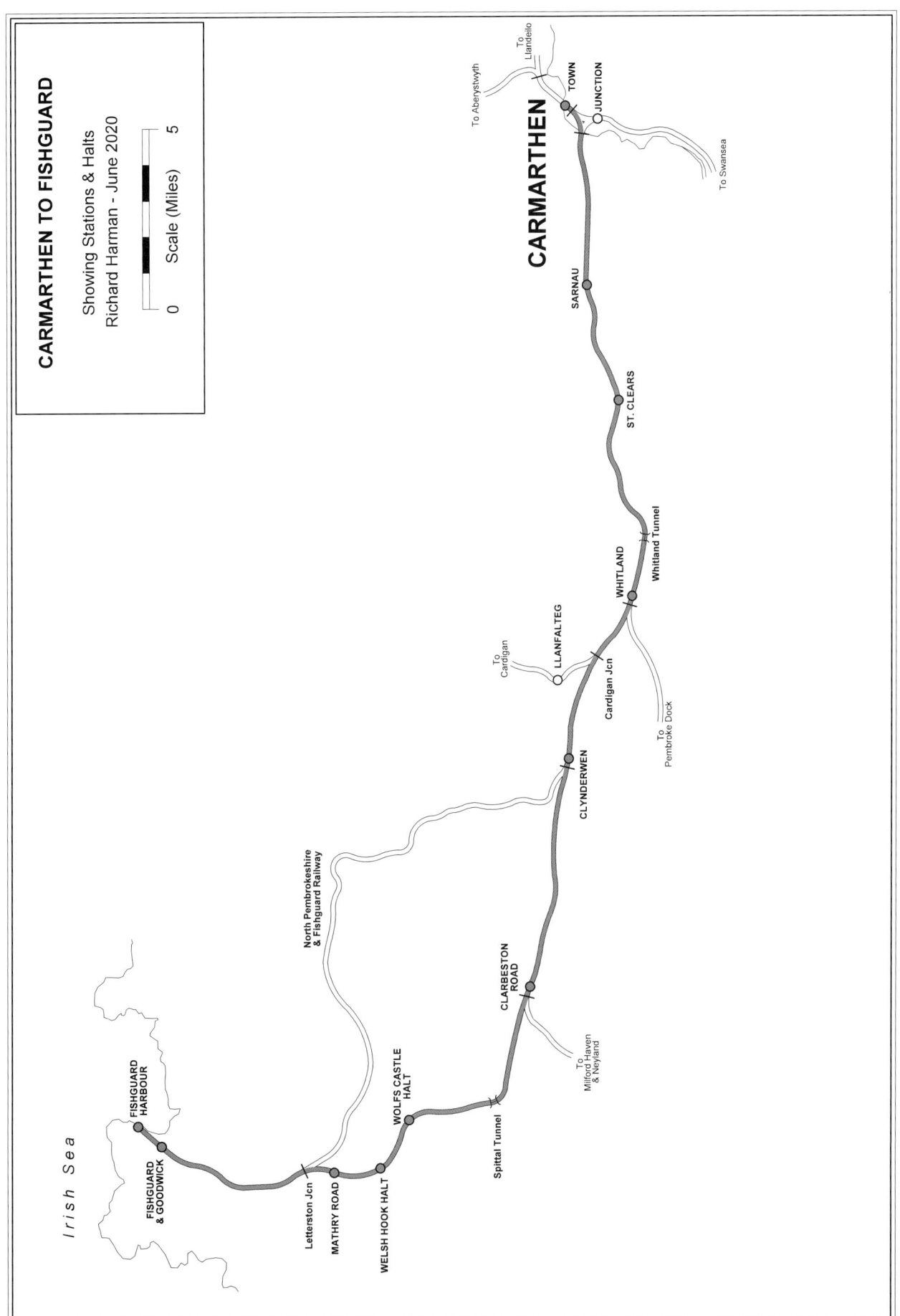

Map of Carmarthen to Fishguard Harbour. (Richard Harman)

INTRODUCTION

DEVELOPMENT OF FISHGUARD HARBOUR

Early Services

The whole nature of the South Wales Main Line in West Wales radically changed with the opening of Fishguard Harbour in 1906. The previous terminus of the line was at New Milford, which then became Neyland, but the opening of the new port of Fishguard Harbour for steamer services across the Irish Sea injected a huge boost to the line, with full length trains running to and from Paddington, calling only at Landore (for Swansea), Cardiff and Newport in Wales, with the latest in motive power, initially the early 4-6-0s, including No. 98, the first of what became the Saints and later Star Class 4-6-0s. Then from 1908, partly no doubt through the good offices of GW Director Ernest Cunard, Transatlantic Liners en route from America to Liverpool began putting in to Fishguard, creating a rivalry between the GWR and LNWR as to who could get passengers to London quicker, though the GWR were bound to win the battle of who got there first.

On the day of opening the new Fishguard Harbour, the steamer services from New Milford (Neyland) to Waterford and Cork ceased and were transferred to Fishguard. Boat trains conveniently left Paddington at 8.45am and pm, arriving at Fishguard Harbour in 5½ hours, in time to work the connecting services out of the steamers from Ireland back to Paddington. The processing of passengers, mails and baggage was very efficiently performed between the train and boat, only fifteen minutes being the allowance between the train arrival and boat departure. New coaching stock was built for the service with coach nameboards in gold lettering on a red background for the day service reading 'Irish Express via Fishguard' and for the night service 'Irish Mail via Fishguard'. Full dining facilities were provided on each service with a Sleeping Car provided on the evening/night service with a ladies' attendant also travelling. Incoming passengers from Ireland who did not wish to be disturbed in the small hours could remain on board until 8am and use a service to Clarbeston Road, from where there was a service from Neyland through to Paddington. Services connected at Cardiff with restaurant car services to and from Birmingham. With four vessels at their disposal, the GWR ran several excursions especially at weekends, including to the Isle of Man, which often carried up to 1,000 passengers.

It has been established that the 3.35am Up Boat Train to Paddington was worked throughout by Fishguard train crew, who lodged and then worked the 8.45am next day back. Fishguard men also worked the afternoon Up Paddington Irish Goods but only as far as Cardiff. I suspect that initially they would have taken over another Old Oak Saint working through to Fishguard on the 8.45pm ex-Paddington, as at that time only Old Oak, of the depots on the route, had 4-6-0 or 4-4-2 engines capable of such top link passenger working, as will now be shown.

When the service began at the end of August 1906, only Old Oak Common possessed engines which could have worked the prime Fishguard boat train traffic. No. 98 is known from photographs to have been involved, the other allocated Old Oak engines at that time being Scots 173/7 (4-6-0s), 180/5/6/9 (4-4-2s), and Saints 2901/2/4/6/8/9/10. If Fishguard train crew worked these services, the Old

Oak engine must have gone through to Fishguard. It would have been a year before Canton had an allocation of Saints that could have performed/shared the working as it was the autumn of 1907 before they received six Saints, their previous allocation being only 4-4-0s, which, though potentially usable between Cardiff and Fishguard, would not have worked such prestige services to/from London.

At this later date, with Fishguard men working the afternoon Up Paddington Irish Goods as far as Canton, it follows that they could then have worked back with a Canton Saint, taking over the 8.45pm ex-Paddington at Cardiff from either an Old Oak or Cardiff Saint. The new Saint on arrival at Fishguard could then have worked the other Up boat train service next day.

Transatlantic Liners

Initially, the first call of the Transatlantic era was by the Booth Line's *Lanfranc* on 2 April 1908, sailing from South America to Liverpool. A non-stop special train to Paddington, leaving at 8.30pm and hauled by Atbara 3381 *Maine* was run, leaving only 50 minutes after the vessel had dropped anchor inside the breakwater. Over the next six months, twelve more calls were made by the Booth Line, though the connecting trains were limited to three coaches as the number of passengers involved ranged only between ten and thirty-four.

The big events were however provided by the calling of the Cunard Liners, the first of which was *Mauretania* on 30 August 1908, a major event at the port, attended by the GWR General Manager James Inglis, involving the running of full-length connecting trains to London, double-headed from Fishguard to Cardiff by City and Flower 4-4-0s with Star Class 4-6-0s on from Cardiff. The GWR grasped this huge publicity advantage with open arms and used every expedient to reduce the journey time to London over that from Liverpool.

When the Cunard liners started calling in at Fishguard en route to Liverpool in August 1908, the first connecting train to depart was for mails, worked throughout by an Atbara 4-4-0. The connecting passenger services required the provision of full length trains and these were worked by two 4-4-0s of the City and Flower Class to Cardiff. The best engines available were selected, not necessarily Canton based. By now, the Star Class had been introduced, replacing the Saints and Scotts on the top passenger services and new Old Oak Common Stars took over at Cardiff, 4021 *King Edward* taking the first train. All engines at this time had to be provided by Canton and Old Oak Common as Fishguard had no allocation other than a few Bulldogs. Crew working for the Transatlantics between Fishguard and Cardiff with the 4-4-0s was probably in the hands of Canton off the incoming engines, this being quite separate from the basic Irish Boat services.

The working of double-headed 4-4-0s dictated that all trains had to call at Cardiff to change these for a 4-6-0, but the 5-7mins involved was anathema to the GWR in its quest to reduce the running time in its battle with the LNWR's timing from Liverpool to Euston. It was perhaps surprising that for a working starting in August 1908, 4-4-0s were preferred to the fleet of Saints now available at Canton, probably influenced by the need for banking from the Harbour to Manorowen. During the autumn of 1907, Canton had received six Saints. By November of that year, Canton sported 2901/18/19/20/27/29, most of which came new from Swindon and during 1908 this was increased by a further four – 171, 173, 2904 and 2921. Yet the working of the Transatlantics west of Cardiff was handed to double-headed 4-4-0s. There seems to be no record of how long the use of 4-4-0s lasted, but one important feature was the decision to run the first passenger service off the liners nonstop to Paddington. By this time, Canton had begun to receive Stars into its allocation, with 4014 *Knight of the Bath* new in March 1908, 4008 *Royal Star* in August 1909 and 4001 *Dog Star* and 4019 *Knight Templar* in March 1910. The presence of these at Canton (as well as the Saints) must surely have affected the working of the double-headed 4-4-0s, as a Star would have been able to work non-stop through to Paddington with the first connecting train, as were Saints on the Irish services. Banking to Manorowen would probably have been involved.

The inference that the Stars must have played a part in the boat train workings is underlined by the fact that in 1913, all the four Canton Stars were transferred to Fishguard, so it may be inferred that by this time, the working of the Transatlantics was at its most efficient with the first connecting service running non-stop to Paddington and with through services to Dover provided for continental passengers. That the Stars worked through to London is proved by the fact that they were recorded at times under repair at Old Oak Common, doubtless worked there by Fishguard crews.

In 1907/8, the GWR had offered 'day' trips to Killarney from Paddington and had run these non-stop from Paddington to Fishguard Harbour. The only available drivers who knew the road both sides of Cardiff were Cardiff Canton and some Fishguard men and the Canton crews worked the specials in company with a Cardiff guard. These crews travelled 'on the cushions' from Cardiff to Paddington, and then took over the five coach train, with an Atbara 4-4-0, next stop Fishguard Harbour, no doubt making themselves heard as they passed Canton depot, even though it was in the very late hours. The five hour journey completed, they made their way back to Cardiff, probably again 'on the cushions' of the Up Irish boat connection at 3.35am ex-Fishguard.

In order to provide for fast non-stop running, water troughs had been provided at Ferryside (east of Carmarthen), Undy (west of the Severn Tunnel) and Goring (west of Reading) and signals so placed and of such a height (e.g. at Clynderwen) to enable drivers to see them from as far back as possible. The Swansea District Line had been opened in 1912 partly to avoid the need for trains to have to negotiate Cockett bank, all reducing the running time for these Boat trains which were the trains of the day, rivalling the West of England expresses run from Paddington.

What the schedules were for these Transatlantic connections is unknown as they could never be timetabled, departing from Fishguard as soon after the docking of the liner as possible. Trains would be wired forward based on the time off Fishguard Harbour with passing times through to destination based on point-to-point times and recovery allowances, so that each Station Master en route could make the necessary arrangements with his signalmen and station staff. A train conveying mail was always the first train to depart, the original power for its three or four vans being an Atbara 4-4-0. The passenger trains would have had to be telegraphed forward with instruction probably that the line must be clear two blocks in advance and that under no circumstances must it be delayed. On account of these features, no times for these trains have ever been published as far as I know, and the only record of their running would have been the driver's and guard's ticket or journal. Signal box records would have recorded passing times but no overall record of their running or performance ever seems to have been available, a surprising feature as they were top of the list as far as GWR trains of that age were concerned.

Neither has it been possible to get proof that these trains actually ran non-stop from Fishguard to Paddington, though many called at Cardiff only. It was presumed that this aspect would have been covered in the GWR Directors' or Chief Operating Officer's Minutes but these are mostly light on detail with many subjects discussed from papers provided by the investigating officer, the Minutes simply recording that his report was accepted, without saying what the detail of the report was. What is known is that in 1906, Fishguard crews were working through to Paddington and that the Fishguard Stars were recorded at Old Oak Common in 1912/13, some undergoing repair there, and this information is available on the engine data sheets, prepared by Bill Peto, former

Fishguard Harbour's glory days were in the period before the First World War when Cunard Liners, en route from America to Liverpool, put in at Fishguard. Here the arrival of the *Mauretania* on 30 August 1909 saw two passenger specials and a mail special, which was first to leave. Here the first passenger special is about to leave behind two City Class 4-4-0s provided by Cardiff Canton depot, the first of which was 3402 *Halifax*. The second special is probably the train on the extreme left. (Author's Collection)

The first special for the Cunard Liner *Mauretania* leaving Platform 2 photographed from the signal box. (Author's Collection)

12 • CARMARTHEN TO FISHGUARD HARBOUR

The first special leaving the station, photographed from ground level. (Author's Collection)

Approaching Goodwick station. (Author's Collection)

The empty stock for the second special is seen drawing into the station from the west end to leave at 3.03pm behind Flowers 4116 *Mignonette* and 4111 *Anemone* which worked the train to Cardiff where a Star Class 4-6-0 took over to Paddington. (Author's Collection)

The Cunard Liner *Mauretania* in all her glory at anchor off Fishguard in 1908. (National Museum of Wales)

Historical Records Officer of the GW Society. What a fantastic period that must have been as enthusiasts awaited the three train liner connections to go thrashing through, first a Mail train, then a non-stop to Paddington, then an intermediate calling train. What records were ever set by these trains will never be known as nothing was ever studied from the drivers' records. The light trains of probably six coaches would have given plenty of opportunity for speeds approaching or perhaps exceeding 100mph; after all, *City of Truro* achieved it on the Plymouth Ocean Mails.

Post 1914 War

With 1912/13 seeing the height of the Fishguard achievement, the onset of the First World War, the dangers posed by German U-boats, and the ultimate development of Southampton, brought an end to liners calling in at Fishguard, and by the time the war was over, Transatlantic liners were moving to Southampton instead of Liverpool, so the exciting era for Fishguard, for South Wales and for the GWR, was ended and Fishguard reverted to its original use, as the port for the passage merely to and from Ireland. This, however, was always fruitful and a good source of passenger and freight income. One of the traffics that was very common was of Irish cattle en route to London's Smithfield market. Great care had to be taken with this traffic which might account for half a dozen or more wagons per day to ensure the wellbeing of the animals, especially if they had already suffered a rough sea crossing, and if any cattle were 'down' the train needed to be stopped at a convenient location so that they could be attended to. A high category freight service was run mid-afternoon through from Fishguard to Paddington with traffic for intermediate points catered for by other services.

Following the end of the war, not only had Fishguard lost the Transatlantic traffic but the declaration of independence by Eire led to a reduction in services. The service to Rosslare became night only connecting out of the 8pm from Paddington (though this gave a better late evening service to South Wales destinations). This gave an arrival at Rosslare at 5.20am with rail connections serving Waterford (7am), Cork (10am), Killarney (12.37pm) and Dublin Kingsbridge (10.55am). In the return direction, it was 11pm from Rosslare with similar Irish rail connections, 3.35am from Fishguard arr. Paddington 9.35am, again giving very useful early journey times from South Wales to London.

The service to Waterford became MWF – 5pm from Paddington, 11.30pm Fishguard, 8.30am Waterford, return from Waterford TThS connecting for Paddington as above arr. 9.35am. The sailing to Cork operated on TThS off the same 5pm from Paddington, the return connecting into a 4.55am (MSX) from Fishguard (8am Cardiff) to Paddington. By 1939, the Down services from Paddington were at 6.55pm and 7.55pm., with the up services still at 3.35am and 4.55am. After the war, the Down service was confined to the 6.55pm ex-Paddington with a 2.55pm on some Summer Saturdays. The late 1950s and early '60s saw the service extended by the addition of a 3.45pm Summer service with the 3.55pm also conveying a Fishguard portion. The expansion of air travel with regular flights from Heathrow and also Cardiff, with journey time a fraction of the former, has produced a huge reduction in rail traffic which has little significance in the rail timetable these days, a mid-morning DMU service from Cardiff sufficing to connect into the Stena Line vessels.

Fishguard depot's workload contracted during the final years of steam as the boat trains were reduced to the 6.55pm ex-Paddington and the 4.55am ex-Fishguard. The Down train was worked by Old Oak Common as a lodging turn to Swansea, the train then taken over by a Landore crew who worked the 3.55 and 4.55am alternately boat train back to Llanelly. The lack of photographs available for this working is of course explained by the fact that it was all in the hours of darkness. Reliefs were run during the summer which gave some involvement to Fishguard engines and men. The 4.25am relief from Fishguard Harbour to Paddington in the late 1950s and early '60s, was booked to change engines at Llanelly where an Old Oak Castle took over and ran non-stop through to London, using the middle road at Cardiff General. In 1959, an Old Oak Common King was diagrammed to take over the 4.55am from Fishguard at Cardiff at 8.15am, but it was a second rate engine provided and no fireworks were recorded. (For a short while the King returned to London on the 8am Capitals United Express, but this was not to the acceptance of the Canton crew and the train was late most days, and so the working was switched back to the 8.15am and an Old Oak crew.)

By the 1950s, there was no interest in running non-stop through to Paddington, which would have probably involved the crew in lodging overnight, when this was being withdrawn wherever possible, though as the reliefs always ran via the Swansea District line, the choice of re-manning or engine change point was either Llanelly or Felin Fran, and both were used in successive timetables. However, in 1960, the engine change at Llanelly was exchanged for a water stop only, as Ferryside water troughs had been taken out in 1960, indicating a through engine from Fishguard to Paddington was still being used. However, the timings were far from exacting at an average of 40mph, and a Hall or Grange could have filled the bill, though Landore Castles were recorded, the train running very late, probably due to weather conditions in the Irish sea. However, in August 1963, two Castles, 5039/55, were allocated to Fishguard, probably with the intention of being provided for what might have been the non-stop reliefs through to Paddington. On 8 September 1963, Fishguard's 5055 was on Old Oak Common shed, apparently having worked the 4.25am relief, so the final year of steam might have ended with some sort of flourish, though unpublicised. When Hymeks replaced steam on the Fishguard workings, there would have been no problem in achieving through running, the main limitation being the crew rostering. By the summer of 1963, Fishguard reliefs provided the only sight of steam on Western Region London expresses other than those on the Worcester line which remained Castle-hauled for that season.

Fishguard depot no longer exists and the only boat connections are run from and to Cardiff with a DMU or 4 coach train.

The Modern Scene

By the 1970s, the market for travel to and from southern Ireland had changed considerably. Air travel was making huge inroads into sea travel, with passengers travelling to Fishguard having to pass Heathrow and Cardiff Airports en route. On the freight side, British Railways ceased to carry cattle traffic from 1962, removing at a stroke a significant portion of the traffic. In 1972, BR pulled out of the small goods traffic and then in 1976 ended their involvement in wagon load traffic, conveying only trainload or block loads of freight, seeing an end to the activities at Severn Tunnel Junction and to a lesser degree Margam. The market for through trains to and from Paddington ceased and these were replaced by a train each day from Cardiff to connect with the sailing to Ireland, though many more passengers travelled to Fishguard by car or coach. This is the case today and my coverage of Fishguard shows lines of road traffic waiting for access to the port, as a short train covers the rail travel.

Elsewhere in the area covered by this book, almost all services are now covered by diesel multiple units, though some use continues to be made of Class 50 diesel engines to work the Fishguard trains. Pleasant relief from the monotony of DMUs is sometimes provided by preserved steam specials with West Wales being a favourite area for some travel companies, who stop off at Carmarthen where facilities are provided for coaling and watering steam engines, which are then dragged on to Fishguard Harbour or Pembroke Dock from where the steam engine then resumes control for the return. Oil services continue from Milford Haven with huge trains of 24 x 100ton tankers running from Robeston into England with return empties, though several other services from Milford Haven have long ceased. It was the practice for HSTs to run through to Pembroke Dock from Paddington on Summer Saturdays and Class 800 IETs have now been approved to continue the service. The days of Carmarthen being a centre of rail activity in the area are now long gone, but hopefully this book, and my previous book Llanelly West to Carmarthen, will show what a place of interest and activity it used to be. I hope readers will enjoy the selection of photographs I have presented.

WEST WALES MILK TRAFFIC

Milk traffic was amongst the most important traffic carried by rail from West Wales, almost all passing directly to London. The traffic evolved through various stages within the milk production and railway industries, passing from barrels, to churns, to tankers, some being of the roll on/roll off variety to facilitate transfer to and from road. There were two centres used in West Wales, at Whitland and Carmarthen. At Whitland, milk for processing was brought in by road tanker and left the premises for London ultimately in rail tanker. At Carmarthen milk was brought in from the area north of Carmarthen directly by rail tanker from stations north of Carmarthen, off the Aberystwyth branch, as well as by road. Three trains per day were scheduled from Whitland to Kensington and one from Carmarthen, though one of the Whitland starters ran in the peak season only.

Milk traffic was carried by rail from the inception of railways in the country and developed through various stages. Initially the normal way of handling large quantities of milk was in open pails but this was unsuitable for rail conveyance for obvious reasons and the first method used was in closed barrels, similar to beer barrels. These were however heavy to move and took much time and effort to load and remove to and from vehicles. From the 1850s, a galvanised conical churn was developed, holding 17 gallons. This was in general use until the 1930s when the mushroom shaped churn, holding 10 gallons, was introduced and remained in use until the late 1960s. All churns carried a label and were often stamped with the owner's details. Special wagons for the conveyance of milk churns were developed as Siphon Cs by the GWR, later enlarged and modified into Siphon J bogie vans. These often had individual side slats missing to create a through draught in the wagon to keep the churns cool and were later developed as louvred sides. Where no cooling from such means was available, ice and dry ice was conveyed in the vans, against the churns.

The 1920s saw the introduction of milk tank wagons, the chassis owned by the railway and the tank by the milk company. The original tank wagons were four wheelers but the sloshing about of the milk at speed often destabilised the wagon leading to some derailments and detracting from the milk quality. This was overcome by the conversion of the four wheel wagons into six wheelers, giving far greater stability in running and this was the design thereafter. The wagons were always vacuum brake fitted and ran as Class 3 when conveyed in full trains. The 3,000 gallons conveyed by each tanker produced trainloads that required to be hauled by passenger class engines. The GWR also used twin-tank milk wagons so that different types of milk might be carried on the same wagon in lesser quantity.

Milk Trains & Formations – Information drawn from 1959-60 Traffic Working Documents.

The working of Milk traffic between West Wales and London was an important revenue-earning activity for the GWR/Western Region. In the late 1950s, four trains were planned each day, three from Whitland, and one from Carmarthen, all running to Kensington, as follows:

Ex-Whitland
    M-S   3.50pm, 5.15pm, 8.30pm
    Suns   4.10pm, 5.25pm, 6.25pm

Ex-Carmarthen
    M-S   6.45pm
    Suns   9.10pm

The volume of traffic to be conveyed fluctuated due to season, availability and demand and was controlled by a Milk Controller at Paddington Headquarters Control, who wired out details to all concerned parties each day as to the trains to run. The 3.50pm ex-Whitland ran every weekday, with a Sunday counterpart. The 8.30pm ran most weekdays but the 5.15pm ran only when required. All trains were booked for Class 7 power throughout which meant Landore Castles to Swansea or Cardiff, and Swindon or Canton Castles or Britannias (in the 1950s and early 60s) on from Cardiff. The 3.50pm ex-Whitland changed engines at Felin Fran on the Swansea District Line to a Swindon Castle off the 1am Paddington to Cardiff and 7.30am Cardiff to Swansea. The 6.45pm Carmarthen was a Carmarthen and Old Oak Common engine on alternate days throughout.

The marshalling instructions for the trains was a combined feature (i.e. not on an individual train basis) and was:

Engine, West Ealing, Wood Lane, Vauxhall, Wandsworth Road, Stewarts Lane, East Croydon, Mottingham, Morden South, Mitre Bridge, Queens Park, Bollo Lane, Cricklewood, Stratford, Ilford, Bow, Brake-Van Kensington

The arrival of the trains at Kensington connected with forwarding services to each of these places.

The empty tanks were returned by the:-

10.35am Kensington to Neyland (often an ex-works engine from Swindon to Canton, even including the odd Stafford Road King which then worked the 9.48pm Cardiff to Crewe Parcels to Shrewsbury). The train was worked on from Cardiff by a high-mileage Canton Class 7 through to Neyland, returning next day with the 3.50pm Milford Haven Fish. The 10.35am Kensington also conveyed empty Fish Vans to Neyland, for cleaning and provision to Milford Haven for outwards fish traffic, and also Gas-Heated Brake Van 116 or 200 for use on Milk trains back from Whitland. The 10.35am Kensington had replaced the 2.2pm ex-Old Oak Common in the mid-1950s.

The 7.20pm (SX) 7.55pm (SO) Wood Lane to Whitland conveyed empty milk tanks for Ffairfach, Llangadog, Carmarthen, Pont Llanio and Whitland with Brake Van 79 or 187. The return Carmarthen area traffic formed the 6.45pm service to Kensington next day.

Odd tanks were routed on weekends via Swindon and a sweeper service ran as required at 4am Marston to Whitland (Suns).

Some empty milk tanks were returned on the 4.30pm Grimsby to Whitland, though the main traffic on this service was fish traffic, the vans continuing on to Neyland after being emptied. There was also an as required service on Monday mornings at 1.15am from Swindon to Whitland which mopped up any surplus vans which had been worked into Swindon on Sundays, other tankers being conveyed on Parcels or Class 2 passenger services as tail traffic.

Returned empty tanks were cleaned at either Carmarthen or Whitland milk depots as appropriate. Though the Whitland traffic was all loaded at Whitland milk depot, the traffic on the 6.45pm ex-Carmarthen had been loaded at Ffairfach, Llangadog and Pont Llanio as well as Carmarthen.

By 1963, the pattern of services had changed and the 6.45pm ex-Carmarthen had disappeared, the traffic all being conveyed on the three Whitland services at 3.50pm, 5.20pm Q and 8.30pm Q.

Though almost all the milk traffic was long distance, there was also a milk service at 4.45am from Neath to Aberdare conveying milk tanks from Ffairfach plus a brake-van which returned at 7.5am to Neath, the milk tanks being collected later in the day from Aberdare by the 3.50pm Pontypool Road to Neath.

An important part of the daily workload for the Whitland pilot was preparing the milk trains to Kensington which left at 3.50pm and 8.30pm. Here No. 1613 shunts the brakevans and two milk tanks in preparation for the services during the afternoon on 22 August 1962. (Gerald T. Robinson)

Running between the milk depot and the sidings to form up the 3.50pm milk service to Kensington, No. 1648 shunts the passenger BV and milk tanks through the Up main platform on 1 June 1961. (L.R. Freeman/ Transport Treasury)

In the early 1950s, there was also a Milk Marketing Board service between Carmarthen and Marshfield at 12.55pm, consisting of 3 Siphons of milk churns, but this had ceased by the later 1950s and been replaced by empty milk tankers supplied in the afternoon and loaded ones removed.

WEST WALES FISH TRAFFIC

Fish traffic was originally conveyed in open wagons, vacuum fitted so that they could be attached to passenger trains or run at express speeds in full trains of fish traffic, on the same basis as milk traffic. To achieve this, fish wagons had a long wheelbase and were later built as or converted to six wheelers to improve stability. By the late 1920s and early '30s, the open wagons had been replaced by vans which initially were conventional box vans with improved ventilation. Later, insulated fish vans were developed (INSULFISH) and these represented the final design for this specialised traffic. Fish traffic was also carried in containers, which did not allow the uninitiated to know what the traffic was! Generally, however, the pungent fish smell gave the game away. I remember travelling on the footplate of the 3.50pm fish train from Milford Haven and dreading each time we stopped as we would be overcome by the aroma.

As part of the Beeching Report into the economics of rail transport in this country, it was decided that fish traffic was uneconomic and from 1964, British Railways stopped carrying this traffic, another victory for road transport! Many of the wagons previously used for fish traffic were subsequently used for parcels traffic.

Milford Haven was one of some seven large fishing ports in the country where fish traffic was moved largely by rail, the largest being Grimsby, Hull, Aberdeen and Fleetwood followed by Milford, Lowestoft and Leith. Though this was an all-the-year-round traffic, there were seasons for specific landings when the number of vans and trains increased. At Milford Haven, as at other fishing ports, the fish was landed into covered sheds on the quayside where the buying and selling took place. The fish was loaded into light wooden boxes and moved swiftly into the waiting fish vans, which were also packed with ice. Traffic was charged on a weight basis and not per van, which latter might have caused overloading as wagons were filled to capacity.

Into the 1950s, there were two or three fish trains per day (M-F) from Milford Haven, the main train being the 3.50pm which for many years ran to Paddington, the 5.20pm Q service to Paddington and the 3.20pm to Manchester via Carmarthen, Llandeilo and the Central Wales line. In the late 1950s, the 3.50pm ran only to Severn Tunnel, connecting there into fast freight services on to destination, but soon reverted to a Paddington destination, until the demise of the traffic in 1964.

By 1959, Milford Haven was still one of the main fish stations in the country, with three afternoon fish services booked out, at 3.50pm to Severn Tunnel Jcn. (previously to Paddington), 5.20pm Q to Paddington, and 3.20pm to Carmarthen.

Returned empty fish vans were fed into Neyland where they were cleaned and then worked to Milford Haven for loading. The trains run reflected supply and demand, obviously including the type of fish landed in season.

The marshalling instructions for the 3.50pm to Severn Tunnel were dependent on whether the 5.20pm to Paddington ran. If the 5.20pm did not run, the 3.50pm was formed:-

Engine, Swansea, Swindon, Paddington, Gloucester, Cardiff, Rhymney, Pontypridd, Merthyr, Newport, Bristol, Bridgwater, Exeter, Kingswear, Plymouth, Penzance, Brake Van (65, 107, 145 or 1144), Sheffield, Salisbury, Weymouth, Bath.

When the 5.20pm to Paddington ran, the 3.50pm was shown to be formed:-

Engine, Swansea, Treherbert, Aberdare, Merthyr, Porth, Bridgwater, Taunton, Exeter, Plymouth, Penzance, Brake Van (65, 107, 145 or 1144), Sheffield, Salisbury, Weymouth, Bath.

The formation of the 5.20pm to Paddington when it ran was as follows:-

Engine, Swindon, Birmingham (Moor St), Nantybwch, Brynmawr, Ebbw Vale, Newport, Gloucester, Bristol, Cardiff, Rhymney, Merthyr, Paddington (Brake Van 98 or 185). At Cardiff on TWO a 6 coach passenger set was attached off the previous day's 9.25pm ex-Paddington.

The variation in destinations probably reflects the market for the different types of fish landed.

By 1963, the 5.20pm Q to Paddington had disappeared and the 3.45pm ex-Milford Haven was shown through to Paddington, instead of Severn Tunnel Jcn.

A 3.20pm service from Milford Haven to Carmarthen conveyed fish traffic for London Midland Region destinations in the Manchester area and was worked on to Llandeilo where it connected with the 5.5pm Pontardulais to Crewe (SX) and 4.25pm ex-Swansea Victoria on SO. A BG Neyland to Manchester was conveyed throughout, returning on the 9.50pm ex-York next day. Parcels traffic from Swansea Victoria to Crewe, Stores Van No. 16 from Llanelli to Crewe (TO), attached also at Llandeilo, and a Stove R from Swansea to Crewe were also conveyed by this Central Wales service.

Empty fish vans were worked to Neyland for cleaning before being supplied to Milford Haven for loading and were conveyed there on the 4.30pm (SX) Grimsby to Whitland which brought loaded fish vans to Cardiff and Swansea which were then sent forward empty, 1.15am (MO) Swindon to Whitland, 10.35am Kensington to Neyland, 4.55pm Weymouth to Neyland (SX), 4am Marston to Whitland (Suns), and the various parcels trains starting at Cardiff for Neyland.

LOCATION ANALYSIS

CARMARTHEN TO CARMARTHEN BRIDGE

Carmarthen was dealt with in detail in my previous book Llanelly West to Carmarthen to which readers are directed. The original loop line which took trains from the west into Carmarthen Town station was constructed by the Pembroke & Tenby Railway, but this was closed in 1872 and retained as a siding. A drawing of the original triangle between Carmarthen Junction (Myrtle Hill SB), Carmarthen Town Station and Carmarthen Bridge, shows the main line running north to the Carmarthen & Cardigan Rly. Station from the northern apex of the triangle, a single line on the east side and a single line with a loop attached on the west side.

With the opening of the new Carmarthen Town station on 1 July 1902 (see previous volume), the triangle was upgraded. The original P&T line and loop were realigned to become Up and Down lines between Carmarthen Town and Carmarthen Bridge, the realignment also affecting the northern main lines of the triangle. The realignment was completed by September 1911, by when a new bridge had been installed. A Down Goods line was created on the south side alongside the northern lines of the triangle and was brought into use at the end of April 1908. In 1922, a cattle wagon cleaning siding and platform were added to facilitate the working of cattle wagons and trains to and from Fishguard Harbour and other points in West Wales. This would have remained in use until the Railways Board ceased to carry cattle in 1962 and was removed in 1978. The level of sidings was gradually reduced at Carmarthen Junction, particularly after the abandonment of wagon load traffic in 1976, and is now only plain Up and Down running line.

The 09.45 Paddington to Pembroke Dock HST *Pembroke Coast Express* leaves Carmarthen for Whitland and Pembroke Dock on 3 August 1991. (Stephen Miles)

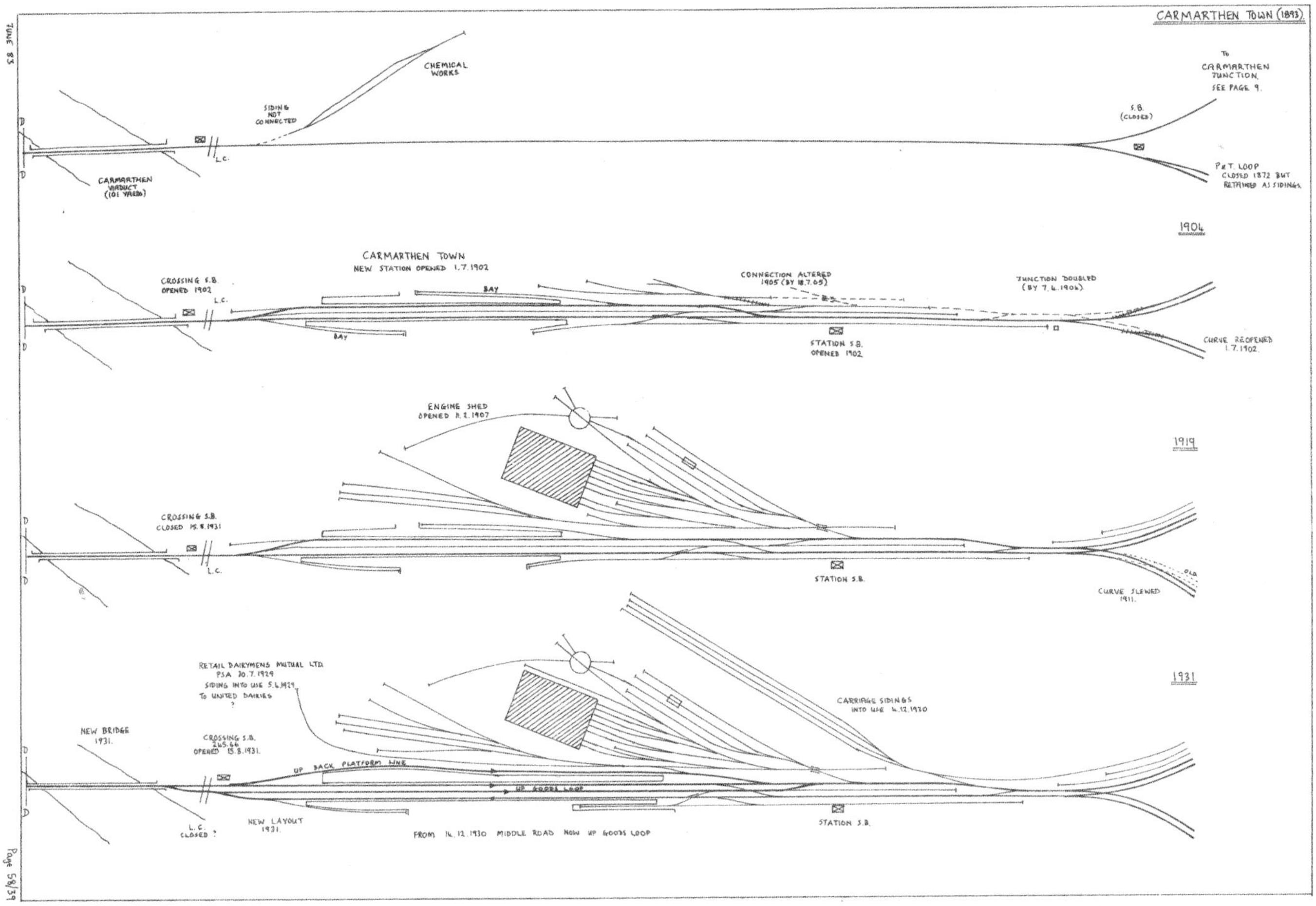

CARMARTHEN TO FISHGUARD HARBOUR • 21

The photographs used show much of the layout of the running lines at Carmarthen, the full position being in this drawing. (Courtesy R.A. Cooke)

The junction at the northern apex of the triangle, the tracks on the left being the Down and Up lines from Carmarthen Bridge, with those on the right to and from Carmarthen Junction. (P.J. Garland/Roger Carpenter)

Rounding the curve towards Carmarthen Bridge, Manor No. 7815 *Fritwell Manor* heads a stopping service beyond Carmarthen in the early 1960s. Coaches can still be seen in the old Junction sidings. (Gerald T. Robinson)

Two views looking through the bridge in 1964 from the west at Llanstephan Crossing towards Carmarthen Bridge SB. The Up loop and stop block on the left were taken out of use in March 1966. Note the Catch Point in the Down Main. (P.J. Garland/Roger Carpenter)

The junction at Carmarthen Bridge as seen in 1964. The lines in the foreground coming out of Carmarthen Town swing east towards the old Junction station and west towards West Wales. (P.J. Garland/Roger Carpenter)

Another view of the bridge from the Carmarthen end showing the tracks to/from Carmarthen station in the foreground as on 5 September 1962. (Alan Jarvis/SLS)

The bascule bridge raised for the passage of ships.

Looking through the bridge, an Up freight train approaching the bridge.

The 10.01 Paddington to Pembroke Dock 1L62 crossing the River Towy on the bascule bridge on 23 June 2018. (Stuart Warr)

A view of the bridge from the river bank. (Stephen Miles)

LLANSTEPHAN CROSSING

Until 1911, the layout here had been Up and Down main lines only, but an Up Goods Loop was brought into use in August 1911 and remained in use until 1966. A temporary Up platform west of the LC and a Down siding (with loading platform) east of the LC were constructed for the Royal Welsh Agricultural Show of 1925. The Down siding later became a mileage siding. The mileage siding was moved to the area previously occupied by the platform on the Up side in 1933, so that the Down siding could be taken over by Cow & Gate in March 1934, later owned by Dairy Crest and Unigate Creameries, the site now closed as a milk processing plant. The Up siding and Up Loop were taken out of use in 1965/66 respectively. Lifting Barriers replaced the crossing gates in March 1965 and the signal box closed in March 1979. The crossing was downgraded to pedestrian use only at that time and the lifting barriers removed.

Llanstephan Crossing looking west from just east of the crossing in May 1964. The Up siding joins the Up main on the left while on the other side of the crossing the Up loop and Down siding can just be seen. (P.J. Garland/Roger Carpenter)

Llanstephan Crossing SB and LC as seen on 15 September 1971. (Garth Tilt)

Another view of Llanstephan Crossing showing the Milk Depot in more detail on 15 September 1971. (Garth Tilt)

Carmarthen Milk Depot with 33016 passing with the 13.05 Swansea to Milford Haven on 14 August 1982. (Stuart Warr)

SARNAU

The station at Sarnau opened in 1888, though there had been an Up siding there since 1883. The platforms at 249m 61ch were of equal length just west of a level crossing and signal box. The Up loop siding was taken out of use in May 1964 and the SB closed in March 1979 when the crossing gates were replaced with lifting barriers.

Sarnau looking west in September 1963. A modest shelter is provided on both platforms with more facilities on the Up platform. (Garth Tilt)

Sarnau looking east in May 1963. The level crossing and signal box are shown, the Up shelter with facilities and Up home signal. (P.J. Garland/Roger Carpenter)

CARMARTHEN TO FISHGUARD HARBOUR • 29

A closer view of Sarnau Signal Box and Level Crossing as on 15 September 1971. (Garth Tilt)

The Up platform building, office and facilities in May 1963. (P.J. Garland/Roger Carpenter)

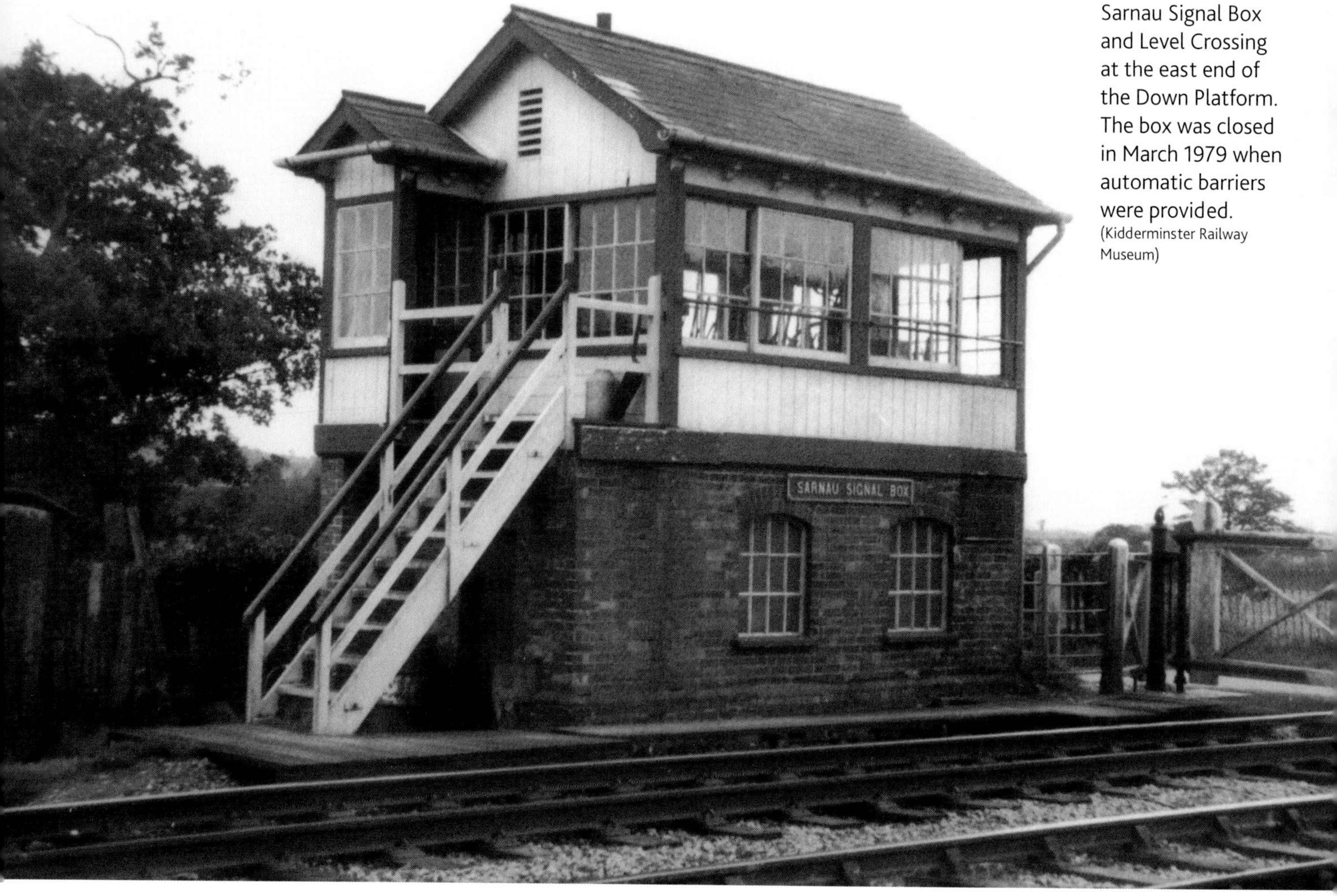

Sarnau Signal Box and Level Crossing at the east end of the Down Platform. The box was closed in March 1979 when automatic barriers were provided. (Kidderminster Railway Museum)

Having just passed Sarnau SB and LC, the RCTS/SLS Special from Swansea to Fishguard runs west behind Cardiff East Dock Grange No. 6859 on 25 September 1965. The siding seen on the left was by then out of use. (Kidderminster Railway Museum)

ST. CLEARS

St.Clears station stood at 253m 14ch. The station consisted of two platforms of equal length with a Goods Shed to the north of the west end of the Up platform, served by a long siding with connections into the Up and Down main lines. A signal box and level crossing were located at the west end of the platforms. Additional sidings were added in 1883 and 1886 to increase the yard accommodation to three sidings west of the goods shed and two to the east, plus a siding to the east and the west of the Down platform. The Down sidings and crossovers into the goods yard were taken out of use in 1966 when the goods shed was closed. The SB closed in November 1978 when the crossing gates were replaced by lifting barriers.

A view of St. Clears station on 8 July 1958 from the west end under the footbridge, showing the reasonably sized station building. (R.M. Casserley)

The west end of St. Clears station platforms with the Goods Shed at the west end of the Up platform. (Lens Of Sutton)

St. Clears looking west in September 1963. (Garth Tilt)

The west end of St. Clears on 29 May 1964 showing the Down siding which stretched back to the level crossing and the connections from the main lines into the goods yard, together with the Up home signal.
(P.J. Garland/Roger Carpenter)

Making a call at St. Clears, Severn Tunnel Junction's No. 6859 *Yiewsley Grange* (name removed) with the RCTS/SLS Special of 25 September 1965 to mark the end of steam haulage over the line. The signal box, level crossing gates and Down starter are featured on the right.
(H.C. Casserley)

The small St. Clears signal box at the west end of the Down platform. The original box was closer to the LC, but was replaced in 1882 by this box, which appears to have lasted until November 1978. (P.J. Garland/Roger Carpenter)

The view west from the station footbridge on 23 May 1963, showing the crossing gates across the main line and goods yard sidings. There are a few wagons on the Down siding, possibly awaiting collection for movement to Whitland, but the main activity is centred on the Up side goods yard which has an interesting population of loaded and empty wagons. At the far end of the yard is a warehouse used for Animal Feeding Stuffs (AFS), a very common sight in yards in West Wales, a highly agricultural area. The wagons on the back road would be awaiting unloading into it. The mineral wagons probably arrived loaded with domestic coal, mainly from the Tondu Valleys. The four loaded Opens nearest the camera appear to be loaded with stone traffic. (P.J. Garland/Roger Carpenter)

A view of St.Clears from the Goods Yard site showing the level crossing and signal box. (Garth Tilt)

A ground-level view from just west of the Up home signal on 25 September 1965, showing the twin entrance goods shed, the shed being empty due to the weekend. (T.J. Edgington)

The station frontage as on 20 October 1904. Whether this was the local taxi service or an event is unclear. (Lens of Sutton)

The frontage of St. Clears station with a Western Welsh bus and private cars waiting. (P.J. Garland/Roger Carpenter)

Another view of the signal box and level crossing. (Kidderminster Railway Museum)

Approaching St. Clears on 22 August 1962, Carmarthen Manor No. 7829 *Ramsbury Manor* with the Up *Pembroke Coast Express*, 1.5pm Pembroke Dock to Paddington. (Gerald T. Robinson)

The six coach 8.55am ex-Paddington (then the Capitals United Express) hauled by Mogul No. 7320 west of St. Clears on 22 August 1962. (Gerald T. Robinson)

Between St. Clears and Whitland was the 189 yard Whitland Tunnel, as seen in this view, these two views on 29 May 1964. Just over three miles west of the tunnel was Ffynnongain LC at 254m 29ch, the gates and signals operated by a ground frame. The ground frame and signals were removed in March 1967, the gates remaining. (P.J. Garland/Roger Carpenter)

Carmarthen RODs were in everyday evidence in this area and here No. 3011 heads a Down Class J service approaching Whitland in August 1950. (E.R. Morten)

St. Clears c1910 with limed cattle wagons prepared here for supply to Fishguard Harbour. (Lens of Sutton)

WHITLAND

Other than in the size of the sidings west of the station, the general appearance of Whitland station changed little from the first drawing available for 1875 to the final one for 1981.

The original Pembroke and Tenby Railway station at Whitland, closed in August 1869, was south of the South Wales Railway, and then the GWR, line, in the area later occupied by the engine shed. The P&T station, which was a dead end consisting of just one platform, probably had two sidings to its north and one to the south, together with an engine shed further to the south.

The GWR station in 1875 consisted of two island platforms, the main lines running between, with bays on the north and south faces of each island. A goods shed was located centrally south of the Down platform with two or three sidings to its south, which merged with the P&T sidings, making it difficult to know which were P&T and which SWR/GWR. A footbridge was provided at the east end of the station (still in place today) with Whitland East SB on the Up side just beyond. Whitland West SB stood at the other end of the station on the Up side controlling the access to and from the Pembroke Dock line. There was one long siding north of the Up main line.

Alterations to layout took place in 1877 when the Down platform was lengthened, two additional sidings provided on the Up side and an additional connection into the engine shed to keep clear of main lines.

By 1910, the siding accommodation west of the station on the north side of the Up main line had been increased, the original siding being lengthened and two new long sidings and one short laid in parallel. On the Down side two new carriage sidings and a Ground Frame to control access to the Down main had been provided by June 1900, the Up side alterations taking place by August 1910.

East of the station a private siding agreement operated by United Dairies began in June 1930; the physical works taking place in August of that year, but the siding did not apparently become operational until 1934.

A view from the footbridge at the east end of the platforms looking west along the station platforms in 1910 with the main block of stone buildings on the Up platform and the goods shed occupying part of the Down platform for which it acts as a shelter. Note the two sections to the Up platform with probably an 850 Class on a train in the station sidings.
(Kidderminster Railway Museum)

By 1950, an Engineer's Pre-Assembly Depot had been created on the Down side west of the station, consisting of four sidings, south of which a new engine turntable was provided in August 1950.

The engine shed closed to steam on 9 September 1963 and closed completely in January 1966.

The Down Siding east of the station was taken over by the Regent Oil Company on 1 November 1965, with a sole use of the siding and loading dock, but the agreement was terminated on 1 August 1968.

2 September 1972 was a landmark day at Whitland as the East and West SBs closed on that day and a new box opened on the Down side at the east end of the station. The Down siding east of the station was taken out of use, the Down Bay (Platform 1) became an Up and Down Bay, and the sidings forming the original Pembroke & Tenby Yard were removed. Further reductions to layout were made in March 1980 so that by 1981, the overall layout was similar to what it had been in 1875, without the P&T element, dictated by the needs of a passenger railway only. Whitland was an important transfer point for parcels traffic and in addition to traffic to and from Pembroke Dock and Cardigan, main line destination traffic to and from Milford Haven, Neyland and Fishguard was handled off many trains. In terms of number of trains, Whitland saw many Class C services, made up of Milk, Fish and Parcels services, as well as passenger trains which until September 1963 ran through to West wales with portion working. Parcels and Mail traffic was conveyed by most passenger and all parcels trains until the 1990s. This has all now been consigned to history but to provide a picture of the position in the Summer of 1957, I have set out details of each train calling, passing, starting and terminating at Whitland in an Appendix, with the Class C services shown in red.

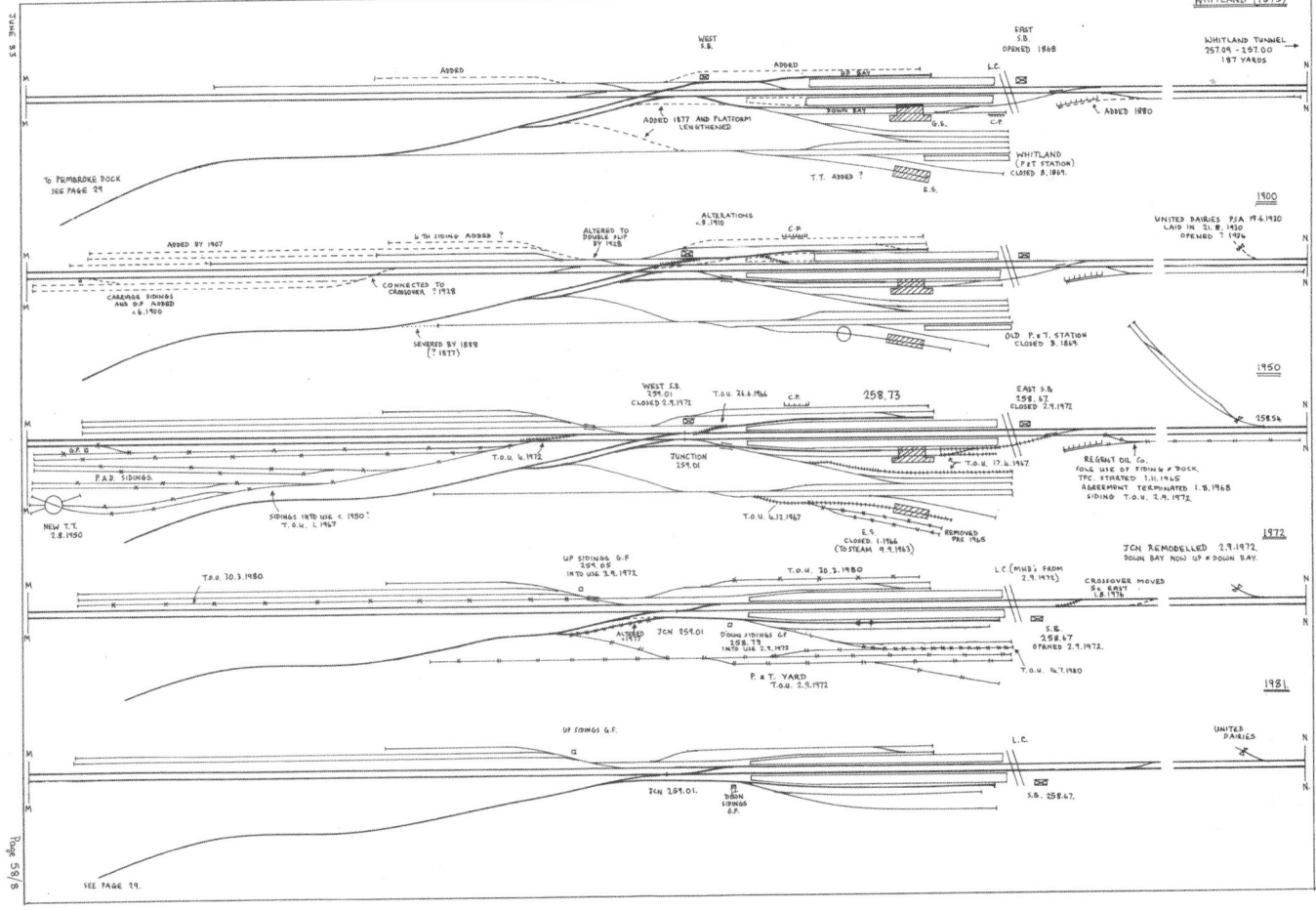

A drawing of the overall layout at Whitland.
(Courtesy R.A. Cooke)

A 1935 view from the Up platform showing the brick and stone facilities block at the east end and the covered waiting area in the middle with a better view of the passenger sheltered area on the Down platform. (Lens of Sutton)

A view from the east end footbridge of the 1959 demolition of the stone and brick built facilities block at the east end of the Up platform. A branch train for either Pembroke Dock or Cardigan is standing in the Down bay while a second train, probably for Neyland, at the Down main platform. (Kidderminster Railway Museum)

A wide angle view of the platforms showing the Up yard on 26 June 1963, as Neyland County No. 1001 *County of Bucks* waits with a Down stopper. (C.M. & J.M. Bentley)

Bulldog 3332 *Pluto* at the west end of the Down platform in the 1930s. *Pluto* was a West Wales engine from 1920 when she was allocated to Landore after a Heavy Repair at Swindon. She moved to Carmarthen in 1923 and to Neyland in 1925, before returning to Landore in 1929. She was one of the unfortunates to be withdrawn early due to an excess of power after the introduction of the Halls and was condemned in 1931. This view is probably when she was a Landore engine from 1929. (Dr Ian C. Allen)

A view of the station from the western end after the 1959 re-building with flat-roofed waiting areas and coaches standing at No. 1 Platform to form a Cardigan or Pembroke Dock service. (R.K. Blencowe Collection)

A view of the platforms on 28 December 1979. (Author's Collection)

The view looking east from the footbridge at the end of the platforms on 24 May 1963. This footbridge served as both a way to cross the platforms and as a means of crossing the road when the level crossing barriers were open for trains to pass. Whitland East SB is shown on the extreme left and on the right, the Down siding with its spur and connection into the Down main can be seen together with the line into the Down bay Platform 1 and the Goods Yard and connections from/to the Up main line. The connection to the Unigate PS is on the Up side just past the advanced starter. (P.J. Garland/Roger Carpenter)

A closer view of Whitland East box and the level crossing with the Unigate Creamery in the background on 24 May 1963. (P.J. Garland/Roger Carpenter)

Whitland East Signal Box on 31 July 1987.
(Colour Rail)

Carmarthen Castle No. 7016 *Chester Castle* runs into Whitland with the 10.5am Cardiff to Neyland Parcels on 1 June 1961, while Neyland County No. 1010 *County of Caernarvon* waits at the Up platform.
(L.R. Freeman/Transport Treasury)

Carmarthen Manor No. 7829 *Ramsbury Manor* runs into Whitland with the 11.55am service from Paddington, which will divide up there between Milford Haven and Neyland, on 1 June 1961.
(L.R. Freeman/Transport Treasury)

The only Modified Hall ever allocated to Neyland, Modified Hall No. 6984 *Owsden Hall*, runs into Whitland with a Down express on 26 June 1963, viewed from the east end of the Up main platform.
(C.M. & J.M. Bentley)

Another view of 6984 *Owsden Hall*, seen heading the 12.05pm Milford Haven to Paddington making the Whitland call, with the fish van attached front which would be detached at Cardiff to go forward on the 4.25pm to Portsmouth. (R.Patterston/Colour Rail)

Carmarthen 2251 Class 0-6-0 No. 2226 approaches Whitland station with a Down Class 9 goods on 5 April 1956. (John Hodge)

Neyland Mogul No. 6347 heads east with an Up express, for Paddington on 5 April 1956, with a view of two sets of crossing gates. (John Hodge)

Landore Castle No. 4081 *Warwick Castle* starts away from Whitland with an Up express in the late 1950s. (G.W. Sharpe Collection)

Neyland County No. 1027 *County of Stafford* starts away from Whitland and passes the East Box with the 2.30pm Neyland to Paddington on 22 August 1962. (Gerald T. Robinson)

Short-term Neyland County No. 1019 *County of Merioneth* heads a Down empty Cattle 27 wagon train, probably after cleaning at Carmarthen, past Whitland East box on 27 May 1961. (Alan Wild)

Neyland County 1027 *County of Stafford* with the Neyland portion of a down service from Paddington as 5571 waits with a connection to Cardigan. (W.A.Camwell/SLS)

Departing with the Neyland portion of the 11.55am ex-Paddington is Neyland County No. 1027 *County of Stafford* on 7 July 1962. (Alan Wild)

Neyland Counties were of course an everyday sight at Whitland working to Carmarthen, Swansea and Cardiff. Here No.1010 *County of Caernarvon* is seen at the Up main line platform with the 2.30pm Neyland to Paddington on 1 June 1961. This would be one of No. 1010's last days in West Wales as she went to Swindon Works in June 1961 and was then transferred to Swindon shed.
(L.R. Freeman/Transport Treasury)

Before becoming the first County to be fitted with a double chimney Neyland County 1009 *County of Carmarthen* at the Up platform with a four coach Neyland portion of an Up London service on 31 July 1951. (R.C. Riley/Transport Treasury)

1027 *County of Stafford* stands at the Up platform with the 2.30pm Neyland to Paddington (7pm Cardiff) in August 1962. (Roger Holmes/Hugh Davies)

Neyland County 1020 *County of Monmouth* waits at the Down main platform with the 8.55am Paddington to Neyland which it will work forward to Neyland on 31 May 1961. (L.R. Freeman/ Transport Treasury)

1027 *County of Stafford* runs into Whitland with a Down service from Paddington which it has taken over at Carmarthen while 1648 waits with a connection to Cardigan. (W.A.Camwell/SLS)

Coming off a Down express is County No. 1027 *County of Stafford* on 12 July 1962. (Alan Wild)

The Old Oak Common Castle No. 7015 *Carn Brea Castle* is probably waiting to work the 3.50pm Whitland to Kensington on 21 September 1962 as it waits alongside Neyland County No. 1014 *County of Glamorgan* which is in the Up yard with three fish vans. (F.K. Davies)

Carmarthen Castle No. 5098 *Clifford Castle* runs through the Up platform with the brakevan for the 3.50pm milk service to Kensington on 31 August 1962. (W.G. Sumner)

In the early morning, Old Oak Common Castle No. 5008 *Raglan Castle* ends its run on the 7.20pm Kensington to Whitland Milk Empties and steams into the Down platform on 31 August 1962. (W.G. Sumner)

Carmarthen, Landore and Canton Class 7 power ran beyond Whitland to Fishguard Harbour, Neyland and Milford Haven, and here Carmarthen Castle No. 5020 *Trematon Castle*, which had enjoyed a high reputation when based at Canton in the pre-Britannia days, waits to go forward on 16 November 1961.
(F.K. Davies)

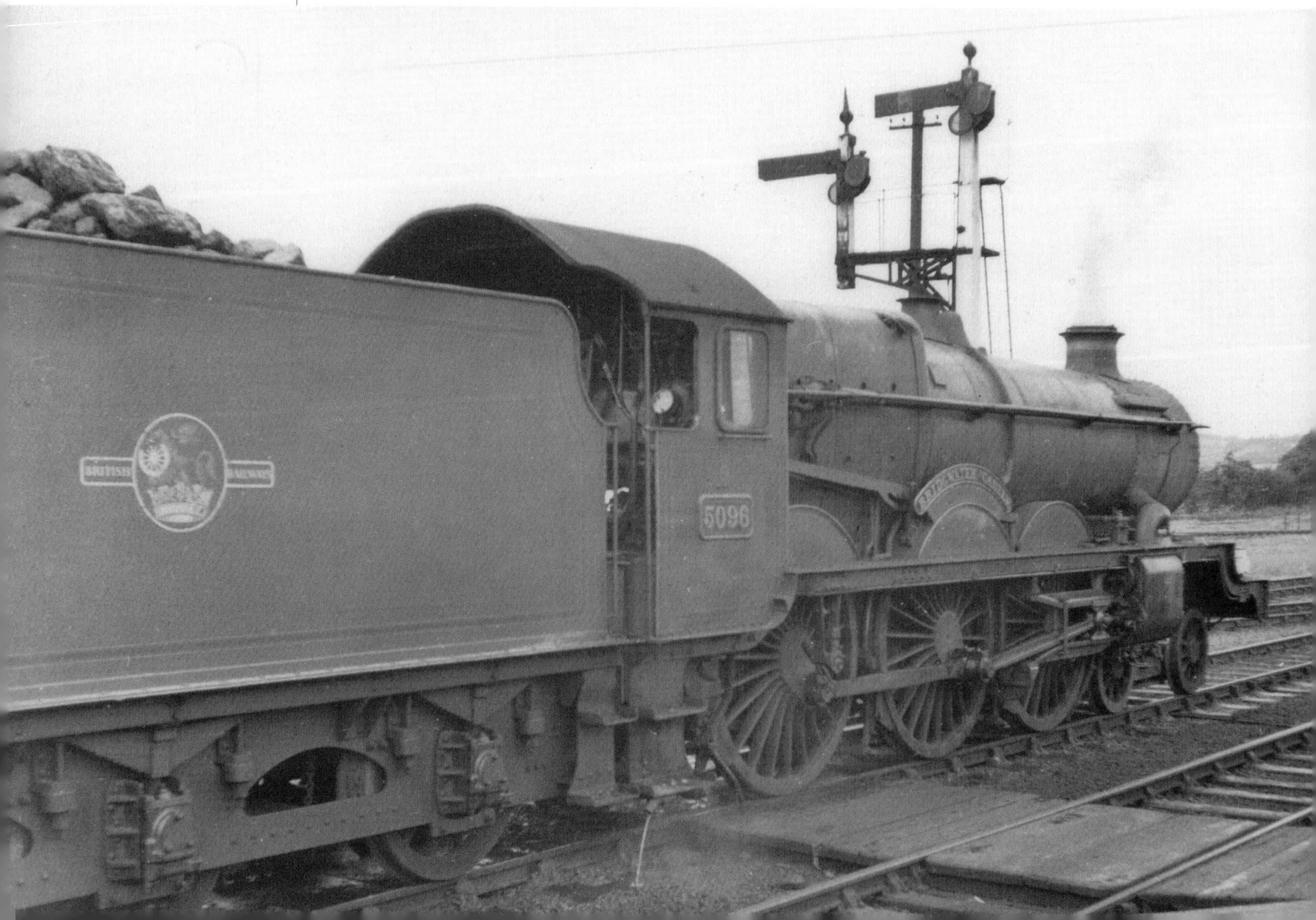

A Canton Castle, No. 5096 *Bridgwater Castle*, awaits the road west with a Down service on 27 September 1961.
(F.K. Davies)

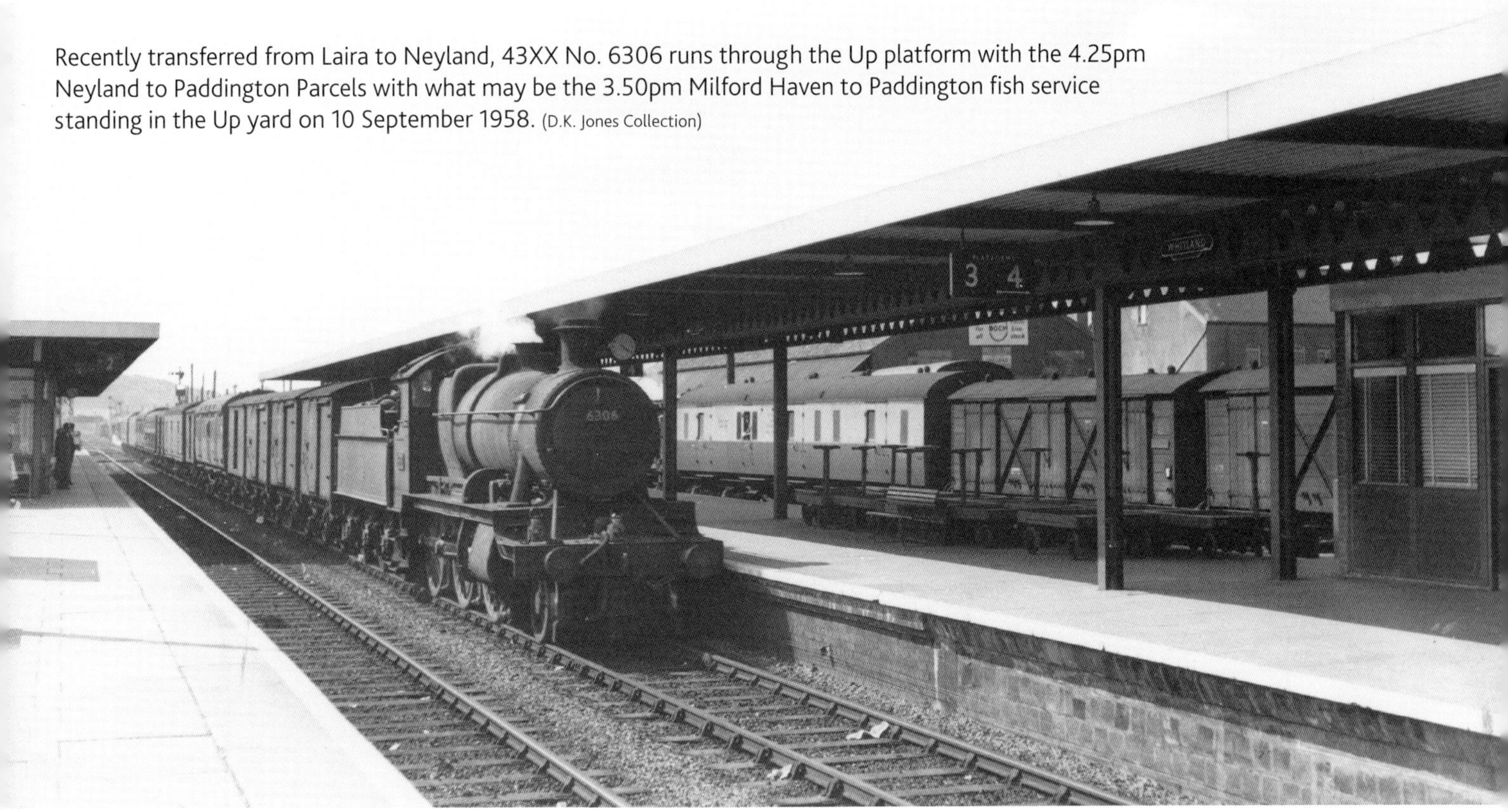

Recently transferred from Laira to Neyland, 43XX No. 6306 runs through the Up platform with the 4.25pm Neyland to Paddington Parcels with what may be the 3.50pm Milford Haven to Paddington fish service standing in the Up yard on 10 September 1958. (D.K. Jones Collection)

After the departure of the Pembroke Dock portion, the remainder of the 8.55am ex-Paddington is two coaches for Neyland which stand at Platform 2 behind Neyland 2-6-0 No. 7318 on 31 August 1962. (W.G. Sumner)

With the station nameboard proudly proclaiming Whitland Junction for Pembroke and Tenby and Cardigan Branches, Neyland 43XX No. 5324 runs through with an eastbound Class F service on 5 April 1956. (John Hodge)

The 43XX 2-6-0 was a useful engine in West Wales with a high route availability, including through to Pembroke Dock. Neyland's No. 6347 stands in the Down branch platform with a Down service in the 1950s. (G.W. Sharpe Collection)

The driver of Neyland's 2-6-0 No. 5353 uses the opportunity to do some oiling as the Pembroke Dock portion is added rear to a Neyland or Milford Haven to Paddington train at the Up platform on 10 May 1958. *(Alec Swain)*

Standing at Platform 1, probably with the 4pm to Cardigan in view of the formation of the train, 4575 Class No. 5550 awaits departure. *(D.K. Jones)*

45xx No. 4558 stands at Platform 1 with the 4pm service to Cardigan, without the Siphon G shown in other pictures of this train, on 22 August 1959.
(R.O. Tuck/Rail Archive Stephenson)

A ground-level view of the Down branch and siding with 45XX No. 4569 waiting with the 4pm service to Cardigan, consisting of a Siphon G and two suburban coaches on 22 August 1962.
(Gerald T. Robinson)

45XX No. 4557 at the Up Main platform 3 in the early 1950s with an arrival from either Cardigan or Pembroke Dock. The stone buildings on the platform date the picture to pre-1959.
(Lens of Sutton)

1628 stands at the Cardigan platform with the late afternoon train to Cardigan with a cattle wagon conveyed behind the engine on 12 September 1952. (R.J. Buckley/Initial Photographics)

Standing ready for departure with a cattle wagon and two coaches, No. 1628 heads a late afternoon service to Cardigan, with the 4.25pm Neyland to Cardiff parcels standing in the Up platform on 12 September 1952. (H.C. Casserley)

The 4200 Class were not a common sight at Whitland though Llanelli engines especially did appear regularly on services from Llandilo Junction. Here Llanelli's No. 4273 runs through the Up platform with an eastbound freight in March 1962. (Colour Rail)

Fishguard Hall No. 5905 *Knowsley Hall* detaches or attaches a freight brakevan off/to what is probably the 10.5am parcels from Cardiff to Neyland at the Down platform in the 1950s. (J. Davenport/Initial Photographics)

There were normally a couple of 81XXs working in the area west of Carmarthen and here 8102 gets the road at the east end of the station with an Up freight for Carmarthen Junction or Llandilo Junction in the 1950s. (R.K. Blencowe Collection)

CARMARTHEN TO FISHGUARD HARBOUR • 61

The last half dozen ROD 2-8-0s were all based at Carmarthen and here No. 3041 runs through the Down platform with a Class J goods in July 1957, shortly before being withdrawn, as 2-6-2T No. 4550 waits in the Down bay with a Cardigan service. (T.J. Edgington)

Whitland based Manor No. 7804 *Baydon Manor* with the three coach through portion of the Up Pembroke Coast Express waiting at the Up main platform on 1 June 1961. The five coach dining portion would be added at Swansea to make an eight coach load for the 2¾ hour journey from Cardiff (dep 5pm) to Paddington, calling at Newport only. (L.R. Freeman/Transport Treasury)

62 • CARMARTHEN TO FISHGUARD HARBOUR

Abundant power for this Up express is provided by Canton Castle 5020 *Tremavton Castle* and Neyland County 1001 *County of Bucks* on 28 July 1951. (Trevor Owen/Colour Rail)

Two Halls head this eastbound service seen waiting at Whitland with Landore's 6912 the train engine. (H.W. Storer/Colour Rail)

Canton Hall No. 6943 *Farnley Hall* waits at the Down platform with a Down Class C service, possibly the 10.5am Cardiff to Neyland, on 24 August 1961. (F.K. Davies)

Carmarthen Hall No. 5938 *Stanley Hall* calls at Whitland with the 12.5pm Milford Haven to Paddington, conveying the van of fish front for Cardiff where it will be transferred to the 4.25pm Cardiff to Portsmouth on 9 July 1962. (Alan Wild)

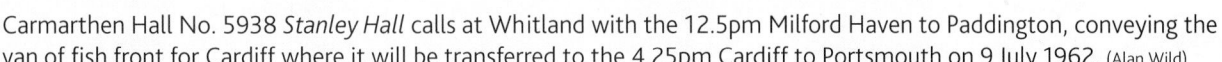

The original stonework buildings on the Up platform are seen in this 5 April 1956 shot of Canton Castle No. 7022 *Hereford Castle* running through the station with the 3.50pm Milford Haven to Paddington Fish which the engine worked through to Canton Sidings having started out the previous evening with the 7.6pm Canton to Milford Haven Fish empties (2.2pm Old Oak Common). (John Hodge)

Whitland based 2251 Class 0-6-0 2263 on main line duty with an Up Class 1 service probably off the Pembroke Dock branch on 28 June 1958. (M.J. Reade/Colour Rail)

CARMARTHEN TO FISHGUARD HARBOUR • 65

One of the highlights of Whitland, on the motive power side, was the double heading of the daily return Cardigan freight which arrived in late afternoon. Here Whitland based 45XXs Nos. 4556/8 arrive at the Up main platform with the train on 5 April 1956. They would then reverse their train into the Up sidings at the west end of the station. (John Hodge)

Nos. 5550 and 1669 propel the return Cardigan freight into the Up sidings on 24 August 1961. (F.K. Davies)

5520 and a 16XX propel the return Cardigan freight into the Up sidings in 1958. (D.K. Jones)

CARMARTHEN TO FISHGUARD HARBOUR • 67

The daily freight from Cardigan on 1 June 1961 double headed by Nos. 4557 and 1669 runs into Platform 3, prior to setting back into the Up sidings. (L.R. Freeman/Transport Treasury)

The power for the return Cardigan freight on 22 August 1962 was a 4575 Class No. 5520 and a 16XX No. 1666, seen propelling the train back into the Up sidings.
(Gerald T. Robinson)

Power in excess. A double headed Cardigan service waits to depart behind 5571 and a 16XX. (W.A. Camwell/SLS)

5571 awaits departure with the Milford Haven portion of a Down service from Paddington with a fish van leading as a 16XX stands at the branch platform with a service to Cardigan.
(W.A.Camwell/SLS)

The view from the west end of the Down platform on 24 May 1963. The connections on the near left are into the station sidings. The Pembroke Dock branch curls away middle left, beyond which are the Down sidings, main lines and Up sidings, with Whitland West box centre right. (P.J. Garland/Roger Carpenter)

A closer view of Whitland West box and surrounding infrastructure on 24 May 1963. (P.J. Garland/Roger Carpenter)

The view from the west end of the Down platform showing the lead to the goods shed and yard, the Cardigan platform and Down main line platform, Whitland West SB and the west end of the Up platforms on 24 September 1963. (P.J. Garland/Roger Carpenter)

Fishguard Hall No. 5905 *Knowsley Hall* pulls away from Whitland with the 9.25am Cardiff to Neyland Parcels on 22 August 1962, though carrying reporting numbers for the 8.55am Paddington to West Wales, probably indicating a change of power allocation at Carmarthen. (Gerald T. Robinson)

Neyland Mogul No. 7320 leaves Whitland with a stopping service to Neyland, which has started out as an express from Paddington on 22 August 1962. (Gerald T. Robinson)

The 4200 and 7200 Class were often to be seen west of Carmarthen, normally Llanelly based engines. Here 4295 heads the 6am Neyland to Llandilo Junction working in Whitland Yard on 17 May 1962.

Another of the Carmarthen RODs 'No. 3024' with an eastbound short goods, probably for Carmarthen Junction or Llandilo Junction on 16 July 1957.
(T.J. Edgington)

Llanelly allocated No. 5903 *Keele Hall* runs through Whitland West under clear signals with what may well be the 2.35pm Fishguard Harbour to Paddington Class C freight on 22 August 1962. (Gerald T. Robinson)

The Manors were a very useful 4-6-0 for West Wales, able to work the more important services on the Pembroke Dock line as well as run to the other main line termini. Here No. 7825 *Lechlade Manor* pulls away from Whitland with a stopping service to Neyland in the late 1950s. (G.W. Sharpe Collection)

Mogul No. 5332 with an eastbound freight in the Up sidings in the 1950s.
(J. Davenport/Initial Photographics)

Dean Goods No. 2474 of Carmarthen shed shunts vans into the Up sidings on 31 July 1951. (R.C. Riley/Transport Treasury)

Fishguard Hall No. 4981 *Abberley Hall* runs through Whitland under clear signals with the 3.35pm Fishguard Harbour to Paddington freight composed of twenty-eight vanfits on 7 July 1962. The engine will work to Canton Sidings where a Canton engine will take over. (Alan Wild)

The Up and Down sidings at Whitland West as seen on 23 May 1963. The Down sidings were used for passenger stock and the Up for freight. (P.J. Garland/Roger Carpenter)

Neyland County No. 1001 *County of Bucks* passes the overgrown Down sidings with a Down express in August 1950. (E.R. Morten)

Leaving Whitland sidings behind the bridge, 2-6-2T No. 4569 sets off for Cardigan with the 4pm service conveying a Siphon G and just one coach on 22 August 1962. (Gerald T. Robinson)

CARMARTHEN TO FISHGUARD HARBOUR • 75

The 3.20pm Milford Haven to Carmarthen to connect for Llandeilo and thence a Central Wales service to the North approaches Whitland behind a grimy Carmarthen Manor 7826 Longworth Manor on 22nd August 1962.
(Gerald T. Robinson)

Looking west at Whitland at the fine selection of semaphore signals still in being on 5 September 1971.
(Garth Tilt)

A Carmarthen to Fishguard Harbour empty stock train passing Whitland Box behind 47501 on 2 August 1980. (Stuart Warr)

Brush Type 4 47473 waits to leave Whitland with the 11.15 Milford Haven to Swansea on 27 September 1982. (Peter Jones)

Brush Type 4 47247 passes the Milk Depot on the approach to Whitland with the Down Trecwn Goods on 27 September 1982. (Peter Jones)

Brush Type 4 47473 approaches Whitland with the 07.44 Cardiff Central to Milford Haven on 27 September 1982. The signal on the left controls exit from the Milk Depot. (Peter Jones)

Brush Type 4 47632 with the 14.27 Milford Haven to Swansea on 4 July 1987. (Stephen Miles)

A Cardiff based unit with an Up service in April 1986. (J. Hazan)

The modern day station at Whitland.
(Philip Halling)

The 10.35 Milford Haven to Penzance at Whitland with DMU 158818 on 22 July 2003.
(Stuart Warr)

Class 37 37232 with a SHARK Brakevan head a return empty ballast train after Sunday engineering work on 11 September 1993.
(Stephen Miles)

CARMARTHEN TO FISHGUARD HARBOUR • 79

The 13.35 Fishguard Harbour to Cardiff approaches Whitland, the four coach Mark 2 def train hauled by 37417 on 6 September 2003. (Stuart Warr)

Passing trains at Whitland. DMU 158822 on an Up service passes Coradia Class 175009 on a Manchester to Milford Haven train on the Down.

The once-familiar sight of the Milk Depot at Whitland East has now gone as Unit 175007 departs on a Milford Haven to Swansea service on 8 August 2012. (Peter Jones)

A Fishguard Harbour to Carmarthen service with DMU 150240 arrives at Whitland on 20 July 2013. (Stuart Warr)

Seen from the footbridge at the east end of the station, Coradia Class 175102, a three coach unit, working the 11.08 Milford Haven to Manchester Piccadilly on 12 March 2014.

A Track Testing train operating from Whitland to Milford Haven and back to Swansea seen at Whitland with 37602 on 9 July 2013. (Stuart Warr)

Network Rail Track Testing train at Whitland hauled by 37421 on 4 March 2016. (Mark Thomas)

CARDIGAN JUNCTION

The junction for the Cardigan branch lay just over two miles west of Whitland at 261m. 14ch. and diverged north-west from the main line to Clynderwen. The junction had a standard layout, trains passing off the main line through a loop on the branch enabling a train to be accepted onto the branch while a train was approaching off the branch. However, with the reduction in traffic over the branch, the junction was singled and the loop removed in 1958, before the branch itself was closed in May 1963. The crossover from the Down Main to the Up to access the branch was not removed until July 1964.

The junction signal box, opened in March 1873, was at first named Taf Vale Jcn. but was renamed Cardigan Junction in 1896. The box was closed in July 1964.

The branch was worked in 'modern' times by 4500 and 4575 Class 2-6-2Ts and 16XX 0-6-0PTs, but in past times had been worked largely by 850 Class 0-6-0Ts, 1076 Class (Buffalos) and other vintage tank types.

The junction as seen on 25 May 1963 showing the signal box and the connection between the Down and Up Main to access the branch. (P.J. Garland/Roger Carpenter)

A close-up on 25 May 1963 of the junction itself and the signal box which was not of conventional design. Note the token collection point at the junction (P.J. Garland/Roger Carpenter)

CARMARTHEN TO FISHGUARD HARBOUR • 83

The branch after singling in 1958 when the loop was removed, as seen on 25 May 1963. (P.J. Garland/Roger Carpenter)

A passenger train from Whitland to Cardigan runs through the crossover from Down to Up Main to access the branch on 27 August 1959. (R.K. Blencowe Collection)

Whitland based 2-6-2T No. 5508 crosses from Down Main to Branch with the last Goods service to Cardigan on 25 May 1963, viewed from the signal box. (P.J. Garland/Roger Carpenter)

No. 5508 joins the branch with the last train northwards, 25 May 1963. Note the straight track between Whitland and Clynderwen. (P.J. Garland/Roger Carpenter)

Passing Llanfalteg West between Whitland and Clynderwen, 33209 heads the 14.50 Swansea to Milford Haven. (Stephen Miles)

CLYNDERWEN

The station at Clynderwen was named Narberth Road until 1 December 1875. It consisted of two off-set platforms with a Goods Depot on the Up side opposite the Down platform. A plan of the layout dated 1876 shows a bay platform on the north side of the Up platform which may have been used for storing the Rosebush branch trains. This was operated by a Ground Frame brought into use in 1877 but discontinued in 1883 when the service was withdrawn.

The Goods Yard consisted of a Goods Shed served by one long siding with a cattle pen at the east end. The siding extended a considerable way westwards with a connection into and from the main lines.

A third running line which was bi-directional ran alongside the Up main and formed the Maenclochog Railway, opened 19 September 1876 and closed 31 December 1882. There was a siding behind the Down platform which was presumably used by these trains and a further siding was added there by 1881.

The original signal box was located at the end of the Down platform from new in April 1876 but was moved in 1877 to be opposite the new connection laid in from the Down Main to the Maenclochog Branch line and from that into the Goods Yard in 1877.

In the layout for 1895, a long siding has been created on the north side of the Maenclochog Branch line, now the North Pembrokeshire and Fishguard Company line, and a group of three Ballast Sidings, probably in connection with the work to be carried out by the latter company, had been laid down on the north side of the goods yard. The Up bay, which

An early view of Clynderwen from the west end showing the elevated signal for high speed running of the Transatlantics. (Lens of Sutton)

had been taken out of use when the Maenclochog line had closed in 1883, was now reinstated and its controlling ground frame transferred from the Down side to the Up, proving that the Up bay was used by Rosebush trains. A long Down refuge siding was created opposite the Up platform and a new signal box opened alongside the old one.

The long crossover from the Down Main to the Branch was removed in December 1940, and the former NP&F branch itself was closed in May 1949, the branch line itself at Clynderwen being retained as a siding. The three ballast sidings mentioned above are now shown simply as yard sidings, but the innermost was removed in 1963, and the outermost shortened. The long siding alongside the former branch line was removed in May 1965, including that portion of it that served the goods shed, which remained served by another siding.

Considerable track and yard rationalisation took place in the mid-1960s and by October 1965, the whole of the goods yard and shed had been removed, the Up and Down bay and the Down refuge siding, so that all that remained were the Up and Down main lines and platforms, the connection between them having been removed in May 1966 and the signal box closing in October 1966, leaving just plain line.

The platforms at Clynderwen were offset to allow the provision of a goods yard on the Up side opposite the Down platform. This is the Up platform which housed the main station facilities on 25 May 1963, showing the reverse crossover between the Up and Down platforms and the start of the connection out of the goods yard. The elevated signal on the Down Main is to permit sighting past the overbridge. The Down Refuge Siding can be seen running into the Down Main. (P.J. Garland/Roger Carpenter)

CARMARTHEN TO FISHGUARD HARBOUR • 87

The Down Platform contained only a passenger shelter with the signal box visible at the far end. The crossover between the Up and Down Main Lines and the connection into the goods yard, the goods shed and the loading dock are clearly seen in this study with the Down starting signal and Up Home or Inner Home. Date is again 25 May 1963. (P.J. Garland/Roger Carpenter)

A track-level view showing the Down Refuge Siding feeding into the Down main on the left and affording a more detailed view of the Up side station facilities. Date is again 25 May 1963. (P.J. Garland/Roger Carpenter)

Two views (from front and rear) of the 45ft Down home signal at Clynderwen, raised to afford maximum viewing for the non-stop services due to the nearby overbridge. The straight track afforded maximum speeds through the area which dated back to the Transatlantic Liner Trains of the 1908-14 era. Note the catch point in the Down Refuge Siding. (P.J. Garland/Roger Carpenter)

A view of Clynderwen station from the overbridge at the east end of the station looking west. (R.K. Blencowe Collection)

The Up side station building and station nameboard as seen on 26 September 1965. (T.J. Edgington)

The compound connection from the Down Main to the Up Main and yard sidings looking west at the west end of the station on 29 May 1964. The siding had been the original Maenclochog branch line and the sidings north of the yard roadway were the original ballast sidings of 1903. The 3 ton Scammell delivery and collection lorry was typical of the time. (P.J. Garland/Roger Carpenter)

An Up four coach veteran service with a Buffalo or 1016 Class in charge waits at Clynderwen in the early years of the century. (Author's Collection)

The 3.50pm Milford Haven to Paddington Fish train hauled by Canton Modified Hall No. 7925 *Westol Hall* runs through the Up platform at Clynderwen on 22 August 1962. (Gerald T. Robinson)

The West Wales portion of an Up London service runs into Clynderwen behind 2-6-0 No. 5385 in August 1961. The Goods Shed activity and the connection from there into the Up main can be clearly seen. The bracket signal had been replaced in the 1963 pictures previously. (D.K. Jones Collection)

Neyland's 61XX No. 6114 between Clarbeston Road and Clynderwen with either the 10.43am Neyland or 11.45am Fishguard Harbour to Carmarthen in June 1962. (M.J. Esau)

The 8.30am Milford Haven to Margam 5F37 freight approaching Clynderwen in charge of Neyland Hall 5903 *Keele Hall* in July 1963. (M.J. Esau)

A new acquisition for Carmarthen in January 1963 after a Heavy Intermediate at Swindon was Manor No. 7815 *Fritwell Manor* seen here at speed approaching Clynderwen with the 12.5pm Milford Haven to Paddington in July 1963. The two Milford Haven to Paddington services at 11.5am and 12.5pm ran nonstop between Haverfordwest and Whitland whereas the Neyland to Paddington services called at Clarbeston Road and Clynderwen. The van of fish conveyed front was detached from the rear of the train at Cardiff for onward conveyance by the 4.25pm Cardiff to Portsmouth. (M.J. Esau)

Another view of Carmarthen Manor No. 7815 between Clarbeston Road and Clynderwen with the 12.5pm Milford Haven to Paddington portion in July 1963. (M.J. Esau)

Neyland County No. 1027 *County of Stafford* approaching its stop at Clynderwen at 3.24pm with the 2.40pm Neyland to Paddington in June 1962. The six coach portion would run through to Swansea where a dining portion would be added for its 5.30pm departure to Paddington. (M.J. Esau)

Affording a good view of the west end of Clynderwen station, showing the goods yard on the left and the Down siding on the right, Llanelly's 2-6-0 No. 6349 runs through with the 7.35am Llandilo Jn. to Fishguard freight in June 1962. (M.J. Esau)

Approaching Clynderwen with what is probably the 2.30pm Fishguard Harbour to Margam, Hall No. 4928 *Gatacre Hall* in June 1962. (M.J. Esau)

Having just left Clynderwen at 3.35pm the Neyland portion of three coaches of the 8.55am ex-Paddington, now running as a Class B, picks up speed behind Neyland 2-6-0 No. 7320 in June 1962. (M.J. Esau)

At speed through Clynderwen, Carmarthen Hall No. 5937 *Stanford Hall* with the 7.55am Neyland to Paddington in June 1962. As can be seen the track sweeps right after Clynderwen, Clarbeston Road being 6½ miles west. (Colour Rail)

Unit 175002 leaves Clynderwen for Milford Haven on 10 August 2012. (Peter Jones)

CARMARTHEN TO FISHGUARD HARBOUR • 95

Unit 175001 leaves Clynderwen with a Fishguard Harbour to Carmarthen service on 10 August 2012. (Peter Jones)

Crompton Class 33 33002 between Clynderwen and Whitland with the 09.30 Milford Haven to Swansea on 27 September 1982. (Peter Jones)

CLARBESTON ROAD

The station at Clarbeston Road was shown on a drawing for 1881 as Up and Down platforms on the route from the east to Haverfordwest, Johnston, Milford Haven and New Milford (Neyland). A signal box was opened west of the station in late 1885, when sidings were laid in on both sides of the main lines near where the route swung left. In this highly agricultural and farming area, cattle pens were provided on the Down siding. Further west lay the abandoned Brunel line to Fishguard of 1851.

With the building of the new line to Fishguard, a new signal box was opened on 23 August 1906, preparatory to the public opening of the route to Fishguard on 30 August. The sidings at the new junction were upgraded and a new Up loop line created running behind the box to accommodate trains recessed for a fast train from Fishguard to pass. The loop was extended east and west as a siding, and other connections provided between the Up and Down main lines.

The Up side station building burnt down on 9 July 1907 and this led to the building of a new station (at 270m 72ch) with a new layout, brought into use on 27 July 1914. The Up loop and extended siding now became an Up bay line for the use of the Fishguard Harbour to Clarbeston Road service. The signal box received a new frame and in February 1917 was renamed East, the West box being on the Haverfordwest branch. When the latter was closed in 1923, the East suffix was dropped.

In 1920, the cattle pens were upgraded into a loading bank for the Clynderwen & District Farmers Association with a Private Siding Agreement dated 10 February. The overall layout remained the same until the post-Beeching era when in 1964 the local service from Fishguard Harbour was withdrawn and all the sidings and most of the crossovers were taken out of use.

The Fishguard line was singled in May 1971 and the junction moved east by two chains in 1982 when the signal box became a panel box for the area.

Clarbeston Road station looking east on 22 May 1963. The Up bay line terminated in the Up platform further west. (P.J. Garland/Roger Carpenter)

CARMARTHEN TO FISHGUARD HARBOUR • 97

Another view from the west end of platforms looking east, showing the Fishguard bay on the left with passengers on the down platform awaiting a service westwards. (PJG/RC)

Clarbeston Road looking west on 22 May 1963. The Down siding and the connection through it to the Down yard is visible with the signal box (centre) and Up loop and running line into the Up bay, with appropriate signalling. (P.J. Garland/Roger Carpenter)

Clarbeston Road Signal Box at the junction between the Fishguard and Haverfordwest routes, the latter seen swinging left on 22 May 1963. The loop and Up bay line run behind the box. (P.J. Garland/Roger Carpenter)

The Up Platform with the Fishguard Bay on the left as on 22 May 1963. (P.J. Garland/Roger Carpenter)

CARMARTHEN TO FISHGUARD HARBOUR • 99

A view west with the local service to Fishguard Harbour in the Bay headed by Fishguard pannier No. 8739 on 22 May 1963. (P.J. Garland/Roger Carpenter)

A view across the tracks to the Up and Down bay where pannier 8739 waits to depart with the 3.35pm to Fishguard on 22 May 1963. (P.J. Garland/Roger Carpenter)

A view from the overbridge at the east end of the station on 2 September 1959 with the train from Fishguard in the Up bay. (R.K. Blencowe Collection)

Looking west on 22 May 1958 with Goodwick's No. 8739 in the bay with the 4.10pm from Fishguard. In the distance wagons can be seen in the Down siding. (N.C. Simmons/Hugh Davies)

A close-up of the local from Fishguard which has just arrived at the Up bay on 2 September 1959 with pannier No. 7747 of Goodwick.
(R.K. Blencowe Collection)

An elevated view of the station on 8 July 1958 with 8739 on the 2.10pm from Fishguard.
(H.C. Casserley)

Goodwick pannier No. 7765 propels its train back to the west end of the station where the engine will run round for the return journey on 11 October 1961. (F.K. Davies)

Taking water at the east end of the Up platform, Goodwick's 57XX No. 9760 with the two coach train from Fishguard on 26 June 1963. (C.M. & J.M. Bentley)

Looking west from the junction with the Neyland line on 22 May 1963. (P.J. Garland/Roger Carpenter)

The 5.25pm to Fishguard Harbour stands at the Down main platform on 2 May 1963 behind pannier 9645 with the usual two coaches. (P.J. Garland/Roger Carpenter)

A view of the station on 12 May 1953 with Neyland Hall No. 5921 *Bingley Hall* running in with the 2.30pm Neyland to Pontypool Road while Goodwick 14XX No. 1431 waits on the 2.10pm from Fishguard Harbour in the Up bay. (T.J. Edgington)

Fishguard's 2251 Class 0-6-0 2223 runs through the station with the 12.35pm Llandilo Jn. to Fishguard Harbour Class F 'which today is only composed of two wagons' on 17 June 1958. (J.F. Aylard/SLS)

A 1955 view with a three coach train departing east while a 14XX sits in the bay with a auto train from Fishguard. (R.K. Blencowe Collection)

A Down stopping service to Neyland waits at Clarbeston Road behind Carmarthen Manor No. 7826 *Longworth Manor* on 2 September 1959. (R.K. Blencowe Collection)

The Up side at Clarbeston Road on 22 May 1958 with Manor 7804 *Baydon Manor* on the 4.25pm Neyland to Cardiff while 8739 waits in the bay with the 4.10pm from Fishguard Harbour. (N.C. Simmons/Hugh Davies)

Recently allocated to Neyland, 43XX No. 6389 waits at the Down platform with the 8am Swansea to Neyland on 8 July 1958. (H.C. Casserley)

A view of the junction with the line from Milford Haven and Neyland taken from a local train from Fishguard on 2 September 1959. (R.K. Blencowe)

Carmarthen Hall No. 5937 *Stanford Hall* starts away from Clarbeston Road with a Neyland to Carmarthen service on 14 September 1961. (M. Whitehouse Collection)

Neyland's County No. 1001 *County of Bucks* stands at the Down platform with a Class B service from Carmarthen, which may well be the Neyland portion of a Down London service, while a Hall runs tender first with a return service to Fishguard in the bay on 26 June 1963. (C.M. & J.M. Bentley)

The exterior of Clarbeston Road station on 8 July 1958, with the famous Casserley car parked outside. (H.C. Casserley)

The bridge at the east end of the platform on 29 May 1964, an ideal vantage point for photographers. (P.J. Garland/Roger Carpenter)

Neyland's 81XX No. 8102 at the east end of the Up platform with the 9.35am Milford Haven to Fishguard service which reversed at Clarbeston Road from 10.6-10.20am, as here on 8 July 1958. (H.C. Casserley)

Manor No. 7814 *Fringford Manor* was only based at Neyland for a six month period from March 1963 and in July is seen running non-stop through Clarbeston Road, with the 12.5pm Milford Haven to Paddington, fast from Haverfordwest to Whitland. (M.J. Esau)

Llanelly Grange No. 6844 *Penhydd Grange* returns east with the 11.15am Fishguard Harbour to Carmarthen freight, balanced off the 7.40am Down freight from Llandlio Jct. in June 1962. The train has just passed through Clarbeston Road and is heading for Clynderwen. (M.J. Esau)

Approaching Clarbeston Road with the 2 coach local from Fishguard Harbour is Carmarthen's 61XX No. 6114 in June 1962. (M.J. Esau)

Clarbeston Road in the early 1960s with Goodwick pannier No. 9760 at rest in the bay with a local from Fishguard, unusually conveying a Siphon G front. (J.S. Gilks)

The 2.30pm Fishguard Harbour to Paddington conveying Irish cattle for Smithfield Market heads through Clarbeston Road behind Goodwick Modified Hall No. 6968 *Woodcock Hall* on 31 August 1962. (W.G. Sumner)

Having been held at the signal seen above the first coach, No. 6118 brings its train from Fishguard into Clarbeston Road on 31 August 1962. (W.G. Sumner)

With the signal off into the Up main line platform, No. 6118 restarts the 5.30pm from Fishguard into Clarbeston Road on 31 August 1962. (W.G. Sumner)

Seen from the fields, the Fishguard Harbour portion of the 11.55am ex-Paddington is worked west at 6.37pm by Carmarthen 61XX No. 6118 on 31 August 1962. (W.G. Sumner)

Carmarthen's 41XX No. 4134 pulls out of Clarbeston Road with a 3 coach stopper which may be the 10.43am Fishguard Harbour to Carmarthen in August 1959. (Colour Rail)

Goodwick 2251 Class 0-6-0 No. 2271 runs into Clarbeston Road with a short train of vans, destined either for Whitland or perhaps Llandilo Jn. in May 1962, shortly before being re-allocated to Machynlleth from where she was withdrawn. (Colour Rail)

West of Clarbeston Road, Neyland 43XX No. 7312 heads the 11.15am Fishguard Harbour to Swansea freight on 12 July 1962. (Alan Wild)

Running into Clarbeston Road, Canton Hall No. 6932 *Burwarton Hall* heads the 7.0am Cardiff General to Neyland Parcels on 12 July 1962. The train will call here from 11.1 to 11.6am and then go forward to Haverfordwest and Neyland. (Alan Wild)

Approaching Clarbeston Road, Goodwick's 2251 Class 0-6-0 No. 3206 heads the short 12.10pm Fishguard to Carmarthen freight on 27 May 1961. (Alan Wild)

Running into Clarbeston Road from the east, Manor No. 7820 *Dinmore Manor* heads the 7.55am Carmarthen to Fishguard service on 27 May 1961. (Alan Wild)

Far from its previous London Division haunts, 61XX No. 6151 runs into Clarbeston Road with the 5.30pm from Fishguard Harbour, now composed of two Mark 1 coaches, on 13 July 1962. (Alan Wild)

This Canton Mogul No. 6345 is an unusual engine to be working this one coach train from probably Milford Haven, seen at Clarbeston Road in May 1962. (Colour Rail)

The present day layout at the west end of Clarbeston Road.

Clarbeston Road Signal Box on 13 November 1976.
(Garth Tilt)

Clarbeston Road Junction for Milford Haven and Fishguard with splitting signal, as seen from the west end of the down platform on 9 November 1985.
(Garth Tilt)

Part of the Clarbeston Road layout coming off the Milford branch with the station in the distance as on 15 October 1969.
(Garth Tilt)

Evoking memories from the past 5051 *Earl Bathurst* with the 16.20 return Fishguard Harbour to Tyseley, The Fishguard Centenary Special, on 19 August 2006. (Stuart Warr)

An Up HST on the 13.50 Fishguard Harbour to Paddington passes a Down excursion hauled by two Class 37s, 37274 and 37686, on 2 August 1997. (Stuart Warr)

The 09.20 Network Rail Track Testing train 1Q13 from Whitland to Milford Haven and then to Swansea, runs through Clarbeston Road Down platform on 9 July 2013, and is then seen west of the station. (Stuart Warr)

CARMARTHEN TO FISHGUARD HARBOUR • 121

A return Fishguard Harbour to Coventry excursion, *The Pembrokeshire Pageant*, runs through Clarbeston Road hauled by 37686 and 37274 on 2 August 1997. At Whitland the train will reverse to Pembroke Dock.
(Stuart Warr)

The 15.53 return excursion to Paddington from Fishguard Harbour crosses the junction at Clarbeston Road behind Western Class diesel D1015 *Western Champion* on 24 September 2005.
(Stuart Warr)

Two views of the 13.35 Fishguard Harbour to Cardiff Central approaching Clarbeston Road composed of Class 37 37425 and 4 Mark 2def air conditioned coaches on 25 September 2004 and 5 September 2003. (Stuart Warr)

CARMARTHEN TO FISHGUARD HARBOUR • 123

The return Northern Belle from Fishguard Harbour crosses the junction at Clarbeston Road headed by Class 47 47790 *Galloway Princess* on 1 March 2014. (Stuart Warr)

When engine and coaches were not provided the train was worked by a Class 150 DMU. Here 150213 works the 13.29 Fishguard Harbour to Cardiff in March 2014.

A Cross Country DMU on a Swansea to Milford Haven service calls at Clarbeston Road on 15 October 1969. (Garth Tilt)

Two Hymeks in multiple with the 14.30 Fishguard Harbour to Margam freight 7F04 passing Clarbeston Road box on 15 October 1969. (Garth Tilt)

Passing the junction with the line to Milford Haven, a Brush Type 4 has plenty of power to spare with three coaches and a van on this Swansea to Fishguard Harbour service on 17 March 1973. (Garth Tilt)

Returning from Fishguard Harbour with the same formation in reverse, approaching Clarbeston Road on 17 March 1973.
(Garth Tilt)

An eastbound oil service of 10 x 100ton tankers passes through Clarbeston Road station, probably heading for Birmingham Albion oil terminal, with the usual Brush Type 4 diesel at the head on 17 March 1973.
(Garth Tilt)

A ballast special heading for the Milford Haven line passes Clarbeston Road SB crossing the junction with the line to Fishguard, behind a Class 37, which may be the Aberdare (Go-Anywhere) turn with ballast from Hirwaun on 6 December 1975.
(Garth Tilt)

A Class 33 crosses through the junction onto the Fishguard lines with a train from Swansea on 9 November 1985. (Garth Tilt)

In a year that saw the restoration of an 8am SO Paddington to Fishguard Harbour boat train, an HST takes the Fishguard line at Clarbeston Road on 3 August 1987. (Garth Tilt)

CARMARTHEN TO FISHGUARD HARBOUR • 127

Two views of the modern Clarbeston Road Up and Down platforms.

SPITTAL TUNNEL, TREFFGARNE, WOLFS CASTLE HALT

The route from Clarbeston Road to Fishguard Harbour was opened for traffic on 29 August 1906, though had been used by contractors and the engineer for some time. The branch opened first as a single line but the section from Letterston Jn. to 20ch west of Wolfs Castle was double and the route on to Clarbeston Road was doubled on 17 December 1906.

Just over three miles west of Clarbeston Road is the 243 yard Spittal Tunnel and initially, there was no station on the new line until the former NP&F station at Goodwick. There had been a contractor's siding and signal box at Treffgarne, opened in August 1906 and closed when the line was doubled in December.

In 1913, a halt was opened at Wolfs Castle at 276m 70ch, consisting of two parallel platforms. In 1925 a private siding was opened for Treffgarne Granite Quarries Ltd. on the south side of the line and a signal box was again provided at 275m 35ch, opened on 1 July 1925 and closed on 17 March 1958, the dates coinciding with the use of the private siding.

The line was singled on 17 May 1971, the Down line being used.

Approaching Spittal Tunnel in June 1962, Fishguard pannier No. 8739 with a local to Clarbeston Road. (M.J. Esau)

Leaving Spittal Tunnel in June 1962, the 10.20am Clarbeston Road to Fishguard Harbour with one Hawksworth coach behind Carmarthen's 43XX No. 5306. (Colour Rail)

Approaching Spittal Tunnel from Clarbeston Road, a Brush Type 4 Diesel Electric heads the westbound Paddington to Fishguard Car Carrier on 14 September 1971. (Garth Tilt)

Two views of Wolfs Castle Halt (For Treffgarne Rocks), the first looking east, the second looking west.
(P.J. Garland/Roger Carpenter, H.C. Casserley)

CARMARTHEN TO FISHGUARD HARBOUR • 131

Approaching the tunnel from the west, a Brush Type 4 with the 14.00 Fishguard Harbour to Swansea on 14 September 1971, after the line had been singled. (Garth Tilt)

The view to the east with 8739 on the 10.20am Fishguard Harbour to Clarbeston Road in the distance. (H.C. Casserley)

132 • CARMARTHEN TO FISHGUARD HARBOUR

A platform level view of the station and overbridge looking west. (H.C. Casserley)

The rather precarious set of steps down from the road to the platform.

The view ahead from a Fishguard Harbour to Clarbeston Road train with Treffgarne Rocks in the distance on 2 September 1959. (R.K. Blencowe Collection)

With a clear view of Treffgarne Rocks ahead, a Fishguard Harbour to Clarbeston Road (eg) 'train' runs east of Wolfs Castle in July 1963. (M.J. Esau)

A returning train from Clarbeston Road has just passed Treffgarne Rocks and is approaching Wolfs Castle in July 1963. (M.J. Esau)

Passing Treffgarne Rocks in June 1962, Fishguard Hall No. 4981 *Abberley Hall* heads the 2.30pm Fishguard Harbour to Paddington freight, with the usual load of cattle (front) and containers. This was a through engine to Cardiff. (M.J. Esau)

Running west near Wolfs Castle in July 1963, a 57XX in charge of a Clarbeston Road to Fishguard Harbour two coach train. (M.J. Esau)

A Fishguard Harbour to Swansea train heads east through Wolfs Castle halt behind a Brush Type 4 diesel on 16 October 1969. (Garth Tilt)

D1648 heads a Fishguard Harbour to Paddington express past Treffgarne Rocks on 23 September 1970. (Garth Tilt)

The 15.45 Fishguard to Paddington passing Treffgarne behind a Brush Type 4 on 4 September 1971. (Garth Tilt)

A Hymek on a Fishguard Harbour to Margam freight rounds the curve at Treffgarne Rocks on 4 September 1971. (Garth Tilt)

WELSH HOOK HALT

Welsh Hook Halt was not opened until 5 May 1924 and consisted of sleepers laid at rail level i.e. no raised platforms.

Welsh Hook Halt looking east on 7 July 1958. (R.M. Casserley)

Welsh Hook Halt looking west on 7 July 1958. The 10.20am Clarbeston Road to Fishguard Harbour has just left behind 81XX No. 8102. (H.C. Casserley)

The Down platform at Welsh Hook Halt seen from a calling train on 22 May 1963. (P.J. Garland/Roger Carpenter)

Passing the former location of Welsh Hook, a Brush Type 4 Diesel Electric heads the 08.00 Paddington to Fishguard Harbour 1F46 on 25 September 1970. (Garth Tilt)

MATHRY ROAD

Opened as Mathry at 280m 44ch on 1 August 1923, the station was renamed Mathry Road on 15 September 1923, and the suffix 'For St David's' was later added to the nameboard, but later removed. The platforms were originally completely offset.

A siding with a goods shed and loading dock was opened on the Up side in May 1923, the Goods facility opening in August. Access to the siding was controlled by a ground frame. By 1925, the siding had been doubled and a signal box was opened at the east end of the station in November 1925. A crossover was provided between the two main lines at the same time and was not removed until September 1965. In about 1935 the Down platform was aligned with the Up.

The Goods siding was taken out of use in December 1963 and the signal box closed in September 1965.

Two views of Mathry Road station on 20 June 1962.
(R.G. Nelson/Terry Walsh)

CARMARTHEN TO FISHGUARD HARBOUR • 139

Above left: The Up Platform with the goods siding and cattle pens behind on 22 May 1963. (P.J. Garland/Roger Carpenter)

Above right: The Up platform with station buildings facing east on 8 July 1958. Note the station nameboard then said Mathry Road For St Davids. (H.C. Casserley)

The east end of the Down platform and signal box seen on 22 May 1963. (P.J. Garland/Roger Carpenter)

Looking west past Mathry Road's home signal on 22 May 1963. (P.J. Garland/Roger Carpenter)

Mathry Road Signal Box and Down Home signal on 2 May 1963. (P.J. Garland/Roger Carpenter)

Goodwick's No. 6116 runs into Mathry Road with the 10.20am Fishguard Harbour to Clarbeston Road service on 13 July 1962. (Alan Wild)

LETTERSTON JUNCTION

The line from Letterston to Goodwick had been opened by the North Pembs. & Fishguard Co. on 1 July 1899 as a single line. The new GW line from Clarbeston Road met this line at Letterston Jn. where a new signal box was opened on

Letterston Jn. signal box with an EBV standing on the line to Letterston and Trecwn RNAD on 2 September 1959.
(R.K. Blencowe Collection)

Returning the token to the machine at Letterston Jn. for the single section from Manorowen on 2 September 1959.
(R.K. Blencowe Collection)

56xx No. 5602 in the Down Goods Loop at Letterston Jn. with a train of containers for Fishguard Harbour on 31 May 1961. (L.R. Freeman/Transport Treasury)

A view east of Letterston Jn. on 22 May 1963. The Down bracket signal controls entry into the Down Goods Loop. The crossover between the Up and Down mains was taken out in June 1966. (P.J. Garland/Roger Carpenter)

5 August 1906 in advance of the start of traffic over the line on the 29th. An Up Goods Loop was provided at Letterston Jn. and this was soon accompanied by a long Down Goods Loop, running beyond the junction by May 1907. In September 1937, a new pair of Up and Down Goods Loops were provided west of the signal box, at which time the box received a new frame.

The DGL west of the box was taken out of use at the end of September 1964, and the Up and Down Goods Loops east of the box were taken out in June 1966. The UGL west of the box became a siding in March 1968 and was removed in May 1972.

The line was singled through to Clarbeston Road in May 1971, but a passing loop was retained at Letterston Jn. The signal box on the Up side of the main line was closed at the end of July 1972 and a new small box opened on the downside at 281m 58ch.

CARMARTHEN TO FISHGUARD HARBOUR • 143

Approaching Letterston Jn. from the west on 22 May 1963. The signal box is seen on the extreme right of the picture, and the triple bracket signal display signals for the Letterston branch, the Up Goods Loop and the Up Main. (P.J. Garland/Roger Carpenter)

A wider angle view of Letterston Junction seen from a Down train on 22 May 1963. (P.J. Garland/Roger Carpenter)

Letterston Jn. SB approaching from the east, showing the Up Goods Loop and Up Main Line on 22 May 1963. (P.J. Garland/Roger Carpenter)

Approaching Letterston Jn. in the Down direction. The Down Goods Loop is holding a rake of vans and minerals, as the signal is off for the Down Main Line on 22 May 1963. (P.J. Garland/Roger Carpenter)

Seen from an Up train on 22 May 1963, Pannier No. 9645 is standing on the Down main awaiting entry to the single line section to Manorowen with empty cattle wagons on the Down Goods Loop. BR had ceased carrying cattle in 1962. The line to Letterston is on the extreme right. (P.J. Garland/Roger Carpenter)

Looking to Fishguard with the NP&F branch on the right on 9 July 1963. (Garth Tilt)

Letterston Junction with 4644 on the 6.32pm Fishguard Harbour to Clarbeston Road on 9 July 1963. (Garth Tilt)

While coming the other way on the same day, the 6.36pm back from Clarbeston Road passing the junction. (Garth Tilt)

The last days of the old box at Letterston Junction as seen on 3 October 1972 with the new box in the distance. (Garth Tilt)

The date is now 10 November 1985; the old box has gone and the new box now controls all movements from the Down side of the line. Note the raised ground position signal replacing the former semaphore signal off the branch. (Garth Tilt)

A view from alongside the new box with an Up DMU to Swansea as a Class 37 waits on the branch with a freight from Trecwn on 28 April 1987. (Garth Tilt)

JORDANSTON HALT (MANOROWEN)

The single line opened by the NP&F was doubled by 5 May 1907. Jordanston Halt at 284m 8ch was opened on 1 October 1923 and consisted of parallel platforms formed of sleepers at rail level. The line was singled on 9 March 1958, the Down line being left as a siding but this too was removed in January 1959.

Manorowen SB, at 285m 8ch, was opened on 5 August 1906 when a loop was brought into use to supplement the single line. The line to Jordanston was doubled on 5 May 1907 but remained single to Goodwick. The line was singled and the signal box closed on 9 March 1958.

Above left: The former Down platform closed when single line operation was begun on 9 March 1958. The line was recovered in January 1959. (R.K. Blencowe Collection)

Above right: Jordanston Halt as on 2 September 1959 with the Up line in use as a single line. (R.K. Blencowe Collection)

Jordanston Halt as seen from an Up train on 22 May 1963. (P.J. Garland/Roger Carpenter)

Goodwick Hall No. 4981 *Abberley Hall* between Fishguard & Goodwick and Jordanston stations with a two coach train which may well be a portion to attach to a Neyland to Paddington service in July 1963. (M.J. Esau)

4981 *Abberley Hall* pilots 5713 on the 3.35pm Fishguard Harbour to Paddington fully fitted freight climbing past Manorowen on 25 June 1959. (J.F.Aylard/SLS)

Canton's 5985 *Mostyn Hall* with the 4.30pm Fishguard Harbour to Paddington service 1A51 heading through Manorowen on 25 June 1959.

Llanelly 8F 48760 heads past Manorowen, banked in the rear, with an eastbound freight.
(J.F.Aylard/SLS)

Class 37 D6836 heads the 2.30pm Fishguard Harbour to Margam 4F01 service, still conveying cattle traffic in June 1963. (J.F.Aylard/SLS)

Climbing out of Fishguard Hall, No. 4962 *Ragley Hall* heads the 2.30pm freight to Paddington conveying four cattle wagons of Irish imports, seen heading for Jordanston in July 1963. (M.J. Esau)

A Fishguard Harbour to Clarbeston Road two coach train powered by Pannier No.9760 on the single line out of Fishguard in July 1963. (M.J. Esau)

Another view of 9760 returning from Clarbeston Road between Manorowen and Goodwick on 5 August 1961. The first coach is a Gresley vehicle, SC32258E.
(J.F. Aylard/SLS)

FISHGUARD & GOODWICK

When opened by the NP&F Co. in 1899, the station was known as Goodwick. It was changed to Fishguard & Goodwick on 1 May 1904. Goodwick was the end of the line from Clynderwen over the NP&F line via Letterston. It consisted of a single platform at the east of the complex (on the south side) for materials for the new Harbour works, but this was closed when no longer required in July 1906.

When the line to Fishguard Harbour opened on 30 August 1906, the station at Fishguard & Goodwick still consisted of just one platform with the main line worked in both directions, the loop line on the south side having become the Up and Down Goods Loop. To the west of the station, the track became double as far as the Harbour station and there was also a Down Avoiding Line south of the mains. A signal box at 287m 49ch was located south of the running lines and mid-way along where a new Down platform would be built, opening on 29 July 1906. A long siding ran behind the box with a connection into the site of the future engine shed.

By 7 August 1907, double line working had been extended to east of the station (287m.38ch), the new Down platform had been built with the signal box just over half way down and the engine shed had been constructed and opened. The shed was only the second example of a Churchward straight shed to be built and consisted of two covered roads with five adjoining sidings and a turntable. To the west of the station there were four loop sidings with access back into the engine shed and adjoining long siding behind the down platform.

By 1925, a third siding had been added to the Up side yard equipped with cattle pens.

The complex underwent little change until the end of steam in West Wales when the engine shed was closed on 9 September 1963. All the sidings in the shed complex were taken out of use by the end of 1963 but the lead to the turntable and the TT itself remained usable until April 1968.

After closure of the passenger station in 1964, the Up platform remained in use in connection with the Car Ferry business, a roll on/roll off arrangement being set up in the yard alongside the platform. The previous Up line and platform became reserved for the car ferry trains with the previous Down line used as the running line, both now bi-directional.

Due to public pressure, the station re-opened in 2012, as have done other stations on lines where the track has been retained for other purposes.

The opening of Fishguard & Goodwick station on 1 August 1899. It closed under the Beeching closures in 1964 (though Motorail facilities continued until 1980) but re-opened on 14 May 2012.

Fishguard & Goodwick station seen on 8 July 1958 with wagons on one of the three sidings in the Up side station yard. (R.M. Casserley)

A view of the west end of the Up platform from a Clarbeston Road to Fishguard Harbour train on 22 May 1963. (P.J. Garland/Roger Carpenter)

In early days the Clarbeston Road service was largely worked by Class 517 0-4-2Ts which worked auto services across the system. Goodwick had three allocated in 1920 and 1930, one of which is doubtless in the picture. (Dr Ian C. Allen/Transport Treasury)

The 2301 Class 0-6-0s found their way onto a variety of workings. Goodwick had none of the class in 1920 but possessed 2371, which appears to be the engine here, in 1930. The train shown could be through to Carmarthen or could be the Clarbeston Road service, as it is composed of veteran GW stock. (Dr Ian C. Allen/Transport Treasury)

CARMARTHEN TO FISHGUARD HARBOUR • 155

Two 14XXs meet at the station in this 1955 shot of Nos. 1431 (Up) and 1452 (Down) on respective auto trains to and from Clarbeston Road. (Great Western Trust)

A return service from Clarbeston Road is worked by this single car auto on 27 June 1955 with engine No. 1431. (F.M. Gates/ SLS Collection)

1431 heading back to the Harbour station with an auto service from Clarbeston Road. (N. Wassell Collection)

Another of Goodwick's auto engines was 1423 seen here working a service to Clarbeston Road. (R.S. Carpenter Colln.)

This elevated view of the platforms, signal box, sidings and engine shed is not dated but is probably from the 1950s. Alongside the engine shed is a rake of empty wagons to go forward to the Harbour sidings with containers on the front, horseboxes and cattle wagons in evidence. (Great Western Trust)

Goodwick pannier No. 9760 runs into the station with a train from the Harbour to Clarbeston Road in August 1961. (D.K. Jones Collection)

Fresh back from works, Goodwick's 7747 works the two coach service to Clarbeston Road seen running into Goodwick station.

A good view of the signal box is provided in this shot of pannier No. 8739 running light along the Down platform at the station in 1960. (R.K. Blencowe Collection)

Two brakevans are propelled through the Down platform by a 57XX in this 1962 shot. (Great Western Trust)

The 11.45am Fishguard Harbour to Carmarthen calls at Goodwick with Carmarthen's 4134 in charge in August 1959. (Colour Rail)

Pulling away from Goodwick station past the engine shed, 9760 works a two coach Clarbeston Road service on 27 May 1961. (Alan Wild)

North of the station was the Brickworks Siding, in use since 1907 first to serve the local Brickworks until 1946 and then transferred to British Anthracite Co. until closed in 1965. Here the 2.35pm Fishguard Harbour to Paddington freight has just passed hauled by Llanelly Hall No. 5903 *Keele Hall*, banked by pannier No. 9666 on 13 July 1962 on the single line. (Alan Wild)

Fishguard Pannier 3637 leaves Goodwick station for the Harbour with a service from Clarbeston Road in June 1958. (J.F. Aylard/SLS)

The main line and sidings to the west of Fishguard & Goodwick station in the 1960s. (R.K. Blencowe Collection)

A Hymek pulls out of the sidings west of the station with a Class 5 freight in the mid-1960s. (R.K. Blencowe Collection)

The 3.35pm Fishguard Harbour to Paddington Freight had a branded brakevan with the entire diagram for the van, one of the few vans running as such on the system. The full details were:-

3.35pm Fishguard Harbour-Paddington

10.10am Paddington-Acton

(Light to Old Oak Common)

1.10am (MX) Old Oak Common-Cardiff

6.10pm Cardiff-Neyland

(Light to Clarbeston Road)

12.30pm Clarbeston Road-Fishguard Harbour (Light)

10.30am (Sun) Llandilo Junc.-Fishguard Harbour

(Light from Clarbeston Road)

9.35pm SO Paddington-Llandilo Junc.

(Light from Old Oak Common)

The detail is commendable but the van was photographed at Milford Haven! *(Alan Wild)*

CARMARTHEN TO FISHGUARD HARBOUR • 163

A 1970 view of what is probably the Fishguard Harbour to Cardiff service passing Goodwick SB.

Fishguard & Goodwick on 19 September 1970.
(Garth Tilt)

Western Class Diesel Hydraulic D 1030 *Western Musketeer* heads the Paddington to Fishguard Car Carrier into Goodwick on 15 September 1971. (Garth Tilt)

The closed Goodwick station on 3 October 1972 with a Class 37 on what is probably a Margam bound freight displaying 4C38. (Garth Tilt)

CARMARTHEN TO FISHGUARD HARBOUR • 165

The Fishguard Harbour to Paddington Car Carrier passing St Mellons West between Cardiff and Newport on 6 August 1965.
(R.O. Tuck/Rail Archive Stephenson)

The new Fishguard & Goodwick platform on 7 August 2012.
(Peter Jones)

The 10.47 service from Cardiff Central to Fishguard Harbour passes the closed station behind 37425 on 25 September 2004. (Stuart Warr)

Western Class DH D1015 *Western Champion* passes the station with the 08.25 Paddington to Fishguard Harbour excursion on 24 September 2005. (Stuart Warr)

CARMARTHEN TO FISHGUARD HARBOUR • 167

Back in business... Sprinter Class 150 150279 works a Fishguard Harbour to Cheltenham service after re-opening.

The new station from an elevated viewpoint as a Class 153 single car calls.

FISHGUARD (GOODWICK) MPD

When Fishguard shed opened at Goodwick in September 1906, the GWR allocated twelve engines, seven being just ex-Swindon Works, and four Bulldogs, three being new engines. There were two Standard Goods and an Aberdare for freight working, four Bulldogs for passenger working and six saddle and pannier tanks for shunting. Two further Bulldogs were allocated ex-Swindon Works in January 1907 but one of the original allocation was re-allocated to Canton in February. The 2021 Class may well have been for the service to Clarbeston Road.

Though the allocation records are maintained as Goodwick, the engines were stencilled FGD.

September 1906 Allocation:-

401 ex-SDN Standard Goods
638 ex-SDN 633 Class
639 ex-SDN 633 Class
652 645 Class 0-6-0ST
686 Standard Goods
1935 Letterston Jan/Cardigan May/ Tenby Aug/Goodwick Sept.
1958 Alloc. Dec. Tenby Jan/Letterston Apl/Whitland Nov.
2130 2021 Class
2635 ex-SDN Aberdare Class
3286 St.Just to CDF Feb 1907
3349 *The Wolf* Alloc. Jan 1907 ex-SDN
3358 *Godolphin* Alloc. Jan 1907 ex-SDN
3710 Unnamed Bulldog New Sept. 1906
3714 ' ' ' '
3729 Weston-super-Mare ' ' '

In 1907 3364 Frank Bibby November, 3411 St.Johns (Atbara) December

1910

By January 1910, the Goodwick allocation had risen to eighteen. There were now two Atbaras, a City, a Flower and three Bulldogs, for passenger working, three Standard Goods and an Aberdare for the freight and four saddle and pannier tanks for shunting. Motor Cars were provided for the Clarbeston Road service. Details were:

Standard Goods 0-6-0 400, 401, 877, 1196
633 Class 0-6-0ST 639
645 Class 0-6-0PT 645
850 Class 0-6-0ST 1218, 1903
Aberdare Class 2-6-0 2608
Bulldog Class 4-4-0 3349 *The Wolf*, 3707 *Francis Mildmay*, 3723
Atbara Class 4-4-0 3379 *Kimberley*, 3387 *Roberts*
City Class 4-4-0 3404 *Lyttleton*
Flower Class 4-4-0 4117 *Narcissus*
Rail Motor Cars 79, 81

Atbaras had first been allocated to Fishguard in 1908 with two (3377/79) arriving in January; both left in July and were replaced by 3382 the same month. No. 3387 arrived in April 1909 but 3382 left in May; No. 3379 came back in September to make the allocation two at year end 1909.

The City, No. 3704 *Lyttleton*, which must have been a prized possession at the time, arrived in January 1908, left in June but returned in September 1909, staying until June 1910 when it left and the class was never again allocated.

Flowers had first arrived at Fishguard in 1908 with 4113 *Hyacinth* in June and 4117 *Narcissus* in July. No. 4113 had departed in October 1909 and 4103 *Calceolaria* arrived in May 1910. There was to be at least one *Flower* on the books at Fishguard until 1921.

The Great Western's desire to improve on the service offered to the Transatlantic Liners began by replacing the double-headed 4-4-0s between Fishguard and Cardiff with a Canton Star. This would have been sometime after March 1908 when the first Star (4014) was allocated to Canton. It was joined in August 1909 by

4008 and then in March 1910 by 4001/19, giving a total of four. It remained as such during 1911/12 but during 1913, they all ceased their involvement with the Fishguard Transatlantic services the main trains which now ran non-stop between Fishguard and Paddington, hauled by Stars based at Fishguard. For this purpose, No. 4039 *Queen Matilda* was based at Fishguard from May 1913, 4001 *Dog Star* from July 1913 and 4000 *North Star* from December of the same year. They were joined by 4026 *King Richard* between July and September 1914 and by 4017 *Knight of Liege* in November 1914. There were thus four allocated during the Summer of 1914.

However with the likelihood of U boat attack in the Irish Sea as the 1914-18 War progressed, the Transatlantic liners ceased to call in at Fishguard and sailed straight to Liverpool. The GW did not remove the Stars from Fishguard immediately for whatever reason; 4000 left in January 1915, and 4039 in November the same year. 4001 left in February 1916 but 4017 remained there until September 1917, doubtless working the Irish Boat Trains either through to Paddington or as far as Cardiff.

During this period, Carmarthen hosted two Stars, 4014 *Knight of the Bath* from March to May 1914 and 4021 *King Edward* from November to December 1914. Whether these were involved in the Fishguard Boat Trains is open to conjecture.

Not only Stars were involved in raising the standards at Fishguard. In December 1911, doubtless also in a move away from 4-4-0 double-heading, two Saints were allocated to Goodwick, Nos. 2937 *Clevedon Court* and 2938 *Corsham Court*, both new ex-Swindon and joined in January 1912 by the new 2940 *Dorney Court*. With 2928 *Saint Sebastian* arriving in February 1913, this brought the allocation to four, but during 1914, this became reduced to two, presumably the reason as for the Stars.

1920

By 1920, things had resumed a much more mundane appearance at Fishguard. With the demand for high speed running consigned to history, the Fishguard Irish services became identified more with incoming Cardiff, Swansea or even Carmarthen engines and Fishguard's sole 4-6-0 was a Saint. Other than this, they still had various main line express duties but these only warranted 4-4-0 power, for which they had two Atbaras, a County, four Flowers and just one Bulldog, the 6ft 8in engines working through to Carmarthen, Swansea and Cardiff, but not to London. The Clarbeston Road services had now passed from steam railmotors to 517 Class 0-4-2Ts, but, probably for freight duties, they now had two of the 4300 Class 2-6-0s. Details of the allocation as at 1 January 1920 were:-

Saint 4-6-0 2941 *Easton Court*
County 4-4-0 3817 *County of Monmouth*
Atbara 4-4-0 4131 *Powerful*, 4136 *Terrible*
Flower 4-4-0 4149 *Auricula*, 4154 *Campanula*, 4156 *Gardenia*, 4168 *Stephanotis*
Bulldog 4-4-0 3306 *Armorel*
4300 Class 2-6-0 4334, 5367
633 Class 0-6-0ST 636
645 Class 0-6-0ST 647, 770, 1016
517 Class 0-4-2T 569, 1435, 1444

Total: 18

The two Atbaras allocated to Fishguard in 1920 remained until March 1922 when one went and the other followed in January 1923. This remained the position until one returned in August 1926 but in December 1927 it left again and the class's association with the depot ceased.

The four Flowers at the depot at the start of 1920 all went by September 1921 and the class was never to return. The County allocated during 1920 remained until August 1921 and that was the end for the class at Fishguard. However, that was not quite the end of the 4-4-0 story at Goodwick as in 1924 a Badminton (No. 4114 *Shelburne*) returned to the depot and remained until July 1927.

The demise of the 4-4-0 at the depot was of course replaced by the arrival of Saints. No. 2941 departed in July 1920 leaving the depot without a Saint and this was the position until three arrived at the end of 1921. Two remained during 1922-3 but 1924 saw a hefty turnover in the class at the depot with six new Saints arriving during the year and four departing. Four new arrivals during 1925 were balanced by four leaving but then in 1926 two new arrivals in February were offset by six leaving the depot so that in October all had gone. 1926 was the year of a complete reorganisation of main line motive power in South Wales, mainly influenced by the number of Kings and Castles now available on the Paddington and West of England route. Stars now returned to Canton for their principal main line turns in support of their fleet of Saints and Saints were concentrated at Landore with up to fifteen allocated in 1928. The diagramming principle for the boat trains in and out of Fishguard was that they were now worked by Canton or Landore engines, with no 4-6-0s allocated to Goodwick.

1930
By 1930, the days of the exotic 4-4-0s, Stars and Saints at Goodwick were long gone and the depot settled down to become a mundane second rate GWR depot with an allocation of sixteen engines that inspired little interest. True, the depot had acquired four of the new Halls, introduced in 1929 but other than that there was nothing to ignite the imagination. The Clarbeston Road and Letterston runs were now in the hands of three 517s but where the load demanded more, there was a Metro 2-4-0T. A Dean Goods had returned and there were now 4 43XX 2-6-0s for intermediate work.

Details of the allocation as at 1 January 1930 were:-

Hall Class 4-6-0 4915 *Condover Hall*,
  4916 *Crumlin Hall*, 4961 *Pyrland Hall*,
4964 *Rodwell Hall*
4300 Class 2-6-0 4340, 4399, 6336, 7302
2301 Class 0-6-0 2371
3600 Class 2-4-0T 3602
1075 Class 0-6-0ST 1597
645 Class 0-6-0PT 647
850 Class 0-6-0PT 861
517 Class 0-4-2T 215, 848, 1456

Total: 16

1940
By 1940, the three 517 Class 0-4-2Ts had been replaced by the new 4800 Class 0-4-2T and the other veteran tanks had been replaced by new 7400 Class panniers. One of the new Granges had been allocated alongside five Halls. Details were:-

Hall Class 4-6-0 4972 *St Brides Hall*,
  5905 *Knowsley Hall*, 5908 *Moreton Hall*, 5928 *Haddon Hall*,
  5929 *Hanham Hall*
Grange Class 4-6-0 6823 *Oakley Grange*
4300 Class 2-6-0 5395, 6344, 6365
5700 Class 0-6-0PT 5716
7400 Class 0-6-0PT 7411, 7412, 7413, 7417
4800 Class 0-4-2T 4824, 4852, 4860

Total: 18

The three Halls Nos. 5905/8/28 were the bane of enthusiasts in England and had been allocated in 1933 and were to remain at Goodwick until the depot closed in September 1963. They only worked as far as Cardiff and it was only when undergoing overhaul at Swindon Works that they went further east, though No. 5908 went to Newton Abbot for a Light Repair in 1947.

No. 5905 (new in 1931) had first been allocated to Swindon, Westbury and

St. Phillips Marsh and went to Goodwick after an Intermediate Repair at Swindon in August 1933. It remained at Goodwick until December 1961 when it entered Swindon Works for a Heavy Intermediate Repair and on release was allocated to Gloucester in February 1962. However, it was re-allocated to Goodwick in July 1962 and survived there until withdrawn in July 1963 when it was sold to Cohens of Morriston for scrap.

No. 5908 (new in 1931) had first been a Swindon engine but after its first Intermediate Repair at Swindon Works had been allocated to Goodwick in January 1933. Though with odd short spells at Landore, Llanelly and Carmarthen and its trip to Newton Abbot Works in 1947, and Caerphilly Works in 1958, it remained at Goodwick until January 1962 when reallocated to St.Phillips Marsh, lasting until July 1963.

No. 5928 had an even more concentrated existence at Goodwick to where it went new in 1933. With only a four month spell at Landore in 1935, it remained at Goodwick until withdrawn in January 1962, and only ever visited Swindon Works outside West and South Wales, which it did on 14 occasions, until it met its demise there on the 15th.

1950

The depot workload had reduced by 1950 by when it could be covered by thirteen engines, four less than in 1940. Three Halls and a Grange remained for the heavier and longer distance mixed traffic, the longest runs being to Cardiff, but all the 2-6-0s had gone.

Details were:-

Hall Class 4-6-0 5905 *Knowsley Hall*, 5908 *Moreton Hall*, 5928 *Haddon Hall*
Grange Class 4-6-0 6823 *Oakley Grange*
5700 Class 0-6-0PT 3637, 5716, 7747, 9602, 9603, 9760
1400 Class 0-4-2T 1423, 1431, 1452

Total 13

The allocation of 14XX auto engines lasted until 1957/8 by when they were all transferred away and the Clarbeston Road service was operated by a 57XX and two coaches, which involved running round at journey end. Three 2251 Class 0-6-0s were allocated to Goodwick by the end of the decade.

1960

The three 2251s allocated at the end of 1959 were soon reduced to one, which left the allocation consisting of five Halls, a 43XX, a 2251 and seven panniers:-

Hall Class 4-6-0 4981 *Abberley Hall*, 5905 *Knowsley Hall*, 5908 *Moreton Hall*, 5928 *Haddon Hall*, 5969 *Honington Hall*
4300 Class 2-6-0 6347
2251 Class 0-6-0 2223 (tsfd. To Ebbw Jn. in August), 2271
5700 Class 0-6-0PT 3637, 4677, 7747, 9602, 9666, 9677, 9760

With the advancing diesel age, two Castles (5039/55) were allocated to Goodwick for nominated diagrams in the Summer 1963 service, but both were moved away in September of that year.

The full details were:-

3.35pm Fishguard Harbour
  – Paddington
10.10am Paddington – Acton
(Light to Old Oak Common)
1.10am (MX) Old Oak Common
  – Cardiff
6.10pm Cardiff – Neyland
(Light to Clarbeston Road)
12.30pm Clarbeston Road – Fishguard Harbour (Light)
10.30am (Sun) Llandilo Junc. –
  Fishguard Harbour
(Light from Clarbeston Road)
9.35pm SO Paddington – Llandilo Junc.
(Light from Old Oak Common)

Two views of the overall layout of Goodwick shed which could be invaluable to modellers, showing the various sidings and connections. The first gives an elevated view of the shed probably in the 1950s with two Halls and three pannier tanks on view.
(Stephenson Locomotive Society)

The second gives a view of the shed from the bank on the north-west side of the depot, showing the tracks leading into the depot as well as the coaling stage and station sidings and running lines on 6 July 1960.
(Stephenson Locomotive Society)

CARMARTHEN TO FISHGUARD HARBOUR • 173

Another view of the depot from a slightly different angle taken from the station footbridge on 27 May 1961. (Alan Wild)

A close-up of the two-road shed and surrounding sidings with a 2251 Class, two Halls and a 57XX on view on 9 June 1962. (R.K. Blencowe Collection)

A view of the shed on 22 May 1958 with a 57XX, 2251 and a Hall in the sidings outside. (N.C. Simmons/Hugh Davies Collection)

Two panniers standing at the entrance to the shed, with part of the shed's side elevation visible on 7 July 1958. (R.M. Casserley)

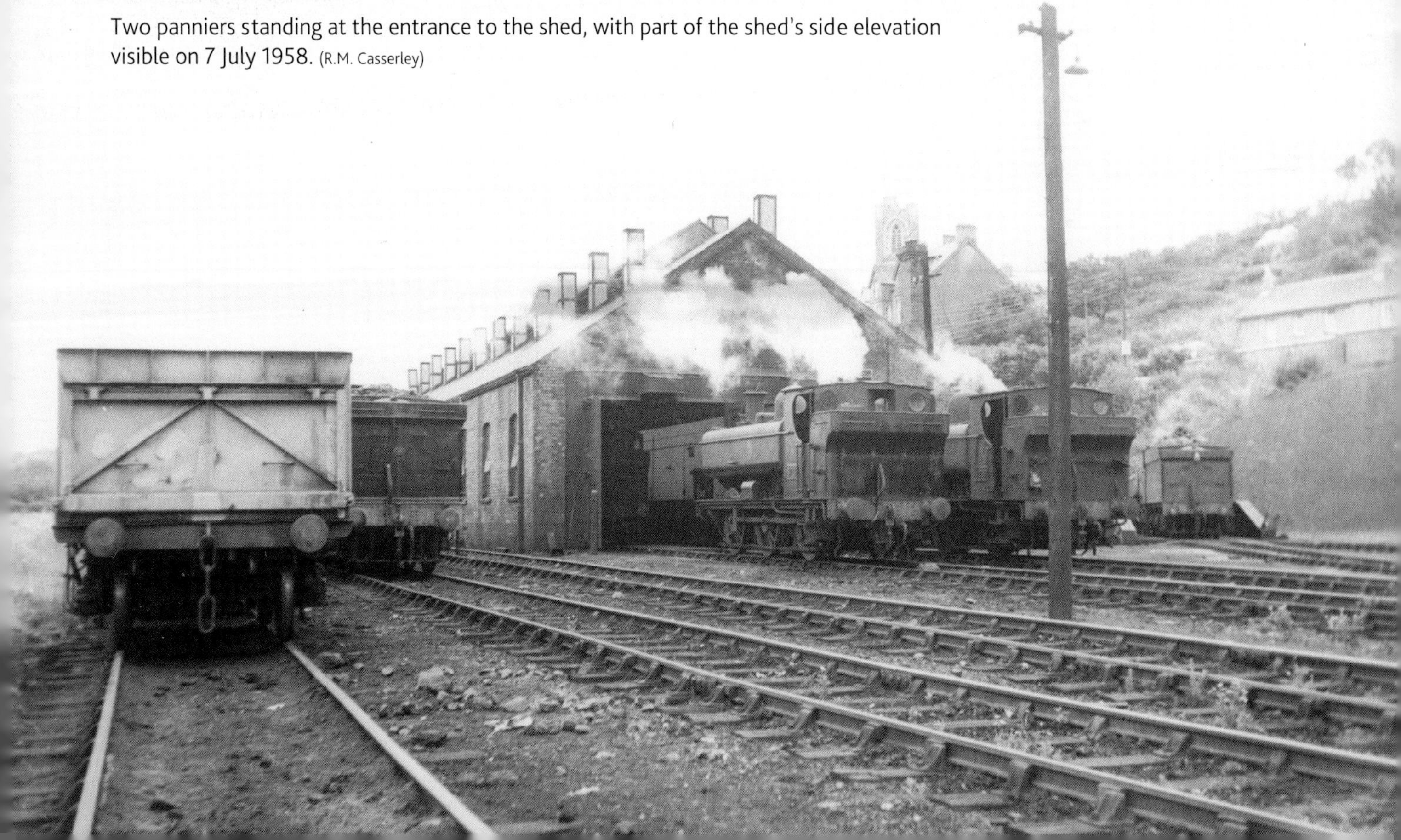

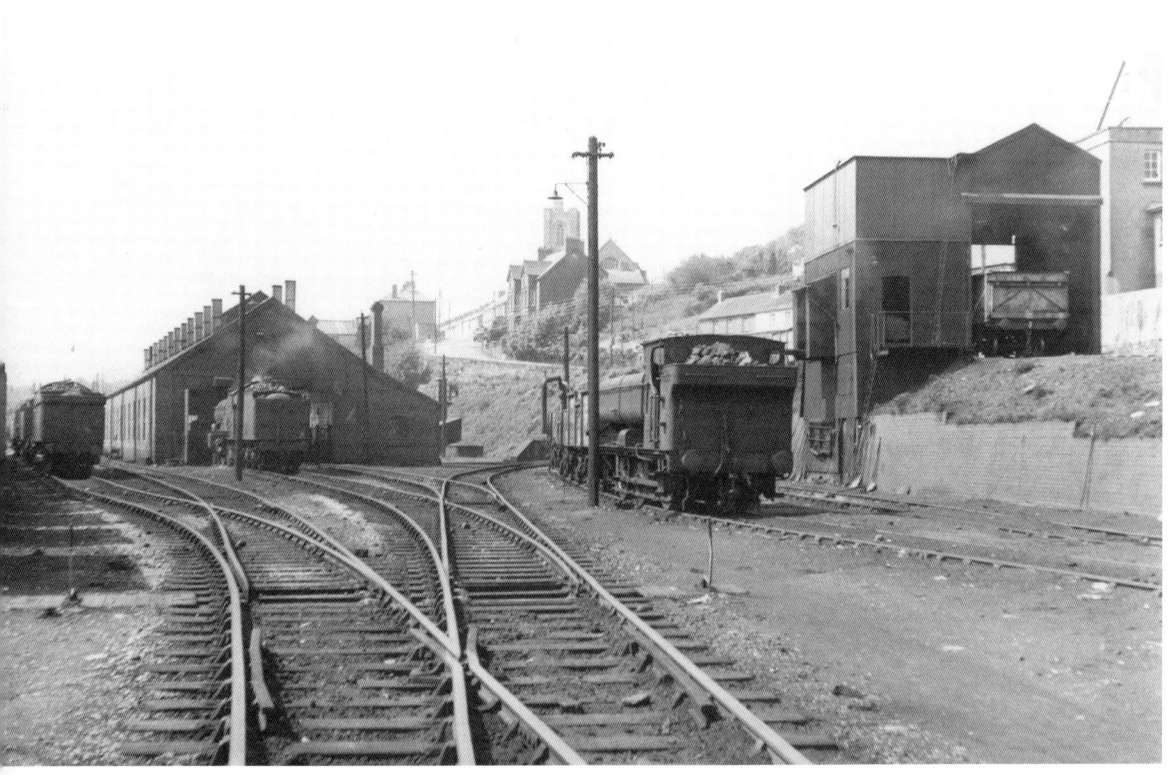

A view of the shed yard with the leads coming into the shed on 25 May 1963 with Hall No. 5905 *Knowsley Hall* in the siding, Llanelly Castle No. 5051 *Earl Bathurst* and pannier No. 8739 in the yard. (E. Wilmshurst)

Goodwick Hall No. 4981 *Abberley Hall* on the turntable on 8 July 1958. (H.C. Casserley)

A view from the north side of the shed showing the turntable and the north face of the shed wall, with Hall No. 5908 *Moreton Hall* on the coal stage road in the early 1950s. (Roger Carpenter Collection)

There were several of the 517 Class 0-4-2Ts based at Goodwick for auto working in the 1920s and 30s. Here No. 215 is seen on the coal stage road probably in the early 1930s. She was withdrawn in January 1934. (Stephenson Locomotive Society)

Goodwick shed on 31 May 1936 with 4860 for working the service to Clarbeston Road. (SLS)

633 Class 0-6-0T 644 at the turntable in April 1929. Probably used on the Clarbeston Road service and on shunting duties, she was withdrawn from Goodwick in 1932.
(Dr Ian C. Allen/Transport Treasury)

Undergoing coaling at the depot on 12 May 1953 is 0-4-2T No. 1431. (T.J. Edgington)

2251s were a useful addition to the Goodwick allocation and here we see two standing in the yard, Nos. 2278 and 2223 in 1959. (Coltas Trust)

CARMARTHEN TO FISHGUARD HARBOUR • 179

Standing at the side of the shed, 3206 with 5928 *Haddon Hall* in 1961.
(M. Harvey/Colour Rail)

2223 with 1423 and 9714 at the shed on 26 August 1954.
(M. Dart/Colour Rail)

Canton Britannia No. 70015 *Apollo* on shed in June 1958. Canton Castles and Britannias worked regularly to Fishguard in the late 1950s, taking over the 6.55pm Paddington to Fishguard at Swansea (off the 5.45pm Cardiff to Swansea) and returning to Cardiff with the 3.55am to Paddington. No. 70015 was one of three Britannias (70015/17/21) transferred from Canton to Trafford Park to work Manchester-Derby-St Pancras services in Summer 1958. (Colour Rail)

Llanelly Castle No. 5039 *Rhuddlan Castle* on shed in September 1963, probably when based at Goodwick. (Colour Rail)

From 1930, Halls were the largest engines allocated to Goodwick, though for a short period in the final months of steam, there was a Castle allocated. Three long term residents 'Nos. 5905/08/28' became the most difficult Halls to see in England during the 1950s and early 60s. Here are three shots of No. 5908 *Moreton Hall* at the shed, the first in 1955, the second on 3 July 1951, and the third on 27 May 1961.
(D.K. Jones Collection X 2, Alan Wild)

5928 *Haddon Hall* alongside the shed on 6 July 1961. (L.W.Rowe/Colour Rail)

Shunting the coal stage road on 27 May 1961 is Goodwick's 57XX No. 4677, after spending many years based at Cardiff Canton. (Alan Wild)

A rear view of 57xx No. 3637 at the shed on 18 August 1960. (F.K. Davies)

In the last year of the GWR, on the coal stage road pannier No. 9602 with 7747 in the yard on 6 April 1947. (F.K. Davies)

4981 *Abberley Hall* outside the 2 road shed on 26 June 1963. (C.M. & J.M. Bentley Collection)

184 • CARMARTHEN TO FISHGUARD HARBOUR

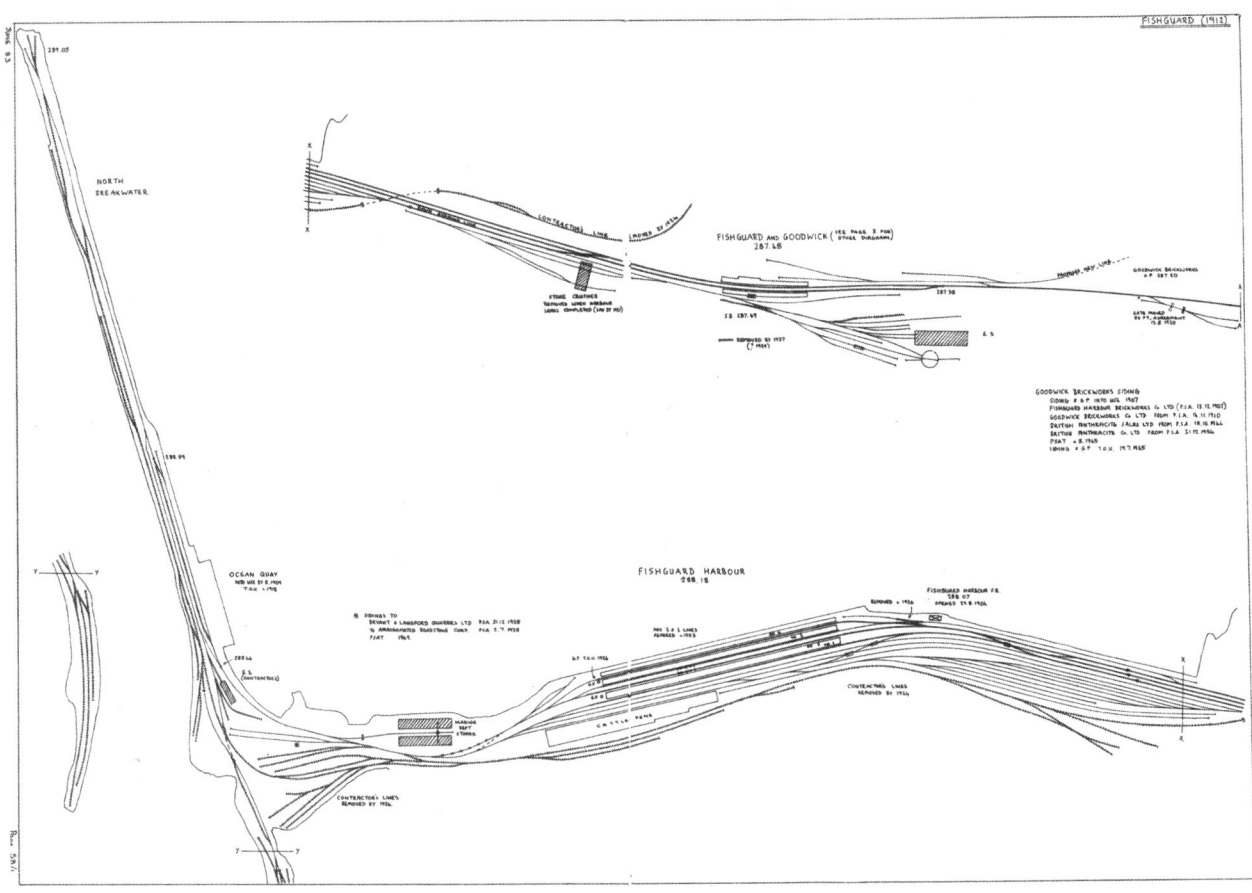
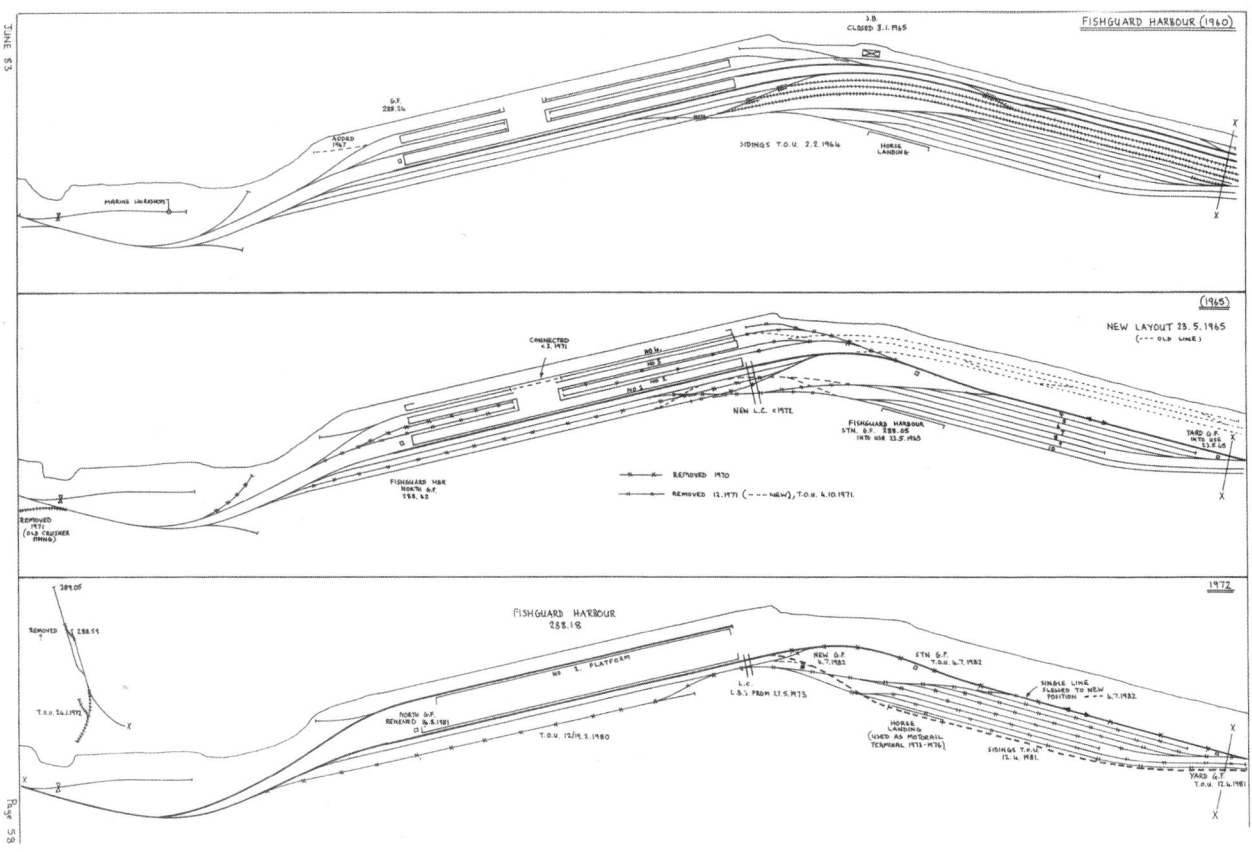

FISHGUARD HARBOUR

When opened in 1906, the approach to Fishguard Harbour from Goodwick station had three running lines, the Up and Down Mains and a Down Loop. On the Up side, there was a loop siding with a spur at the north end and on the Down two further long loop sidings running right down to the station and cattle pens. South of these was a nest of five loop sidings, alongside which was a further nest of three sidings stop-blocked at the north end. South of these were four contractors' sidings, which remained in position until removed in 1924.

All these lines were on the straight from Goodwick station with the signal box on the Up side just before the lines swung left into the platforms. These originally consisted of two long island platforms with a further narrower platform alongside the harbour. On the north side of the complex stood a large cattle pen with underground access for the cattle from the ships, with loading facilities on the south side. Vessels docked alongside the platforms.

To the west of the platforms were large rail connected Marine Dept. Stores, south of which were further contractors' sidings again not removed until 1924. The line then swung south-west alongside the Ocean Quay, brought into use by August 1909 but taken out of use around 1918. The line continued for a further quarter of a mile to the North Breakwater with contractors' lines alongside.

Significant alterations were made to the platform area in 1960 when through passenger access at platform level was made just over half way along the platforms, the effect being to keep the main platform on the south side as a full length platform and to convert the inner platforms to bays. By now a horse loading area had been constructed on the southernmost of the approach sidings but three of the long loop sidings towards Goodwick were taken out of use in February 1964.

Wholesale alterations were made in 1965 when the signal box was closed in January and the previous main line access tracks were taken out of use, access to the terminal now being by a bi-directional single line, with seven sidings retained on the south side. A ground frame located between the running lines and sidings at the east end, quite close to the location of the previous signal box, located at 288m 5ch, then covered all movements and was brought into use on 23 May 1965.

Further platform-serving track was taken out of use in 1970/1 when only the main platform (No. 1) road was left in being. A new level crossing was installed at the east end of the complex in 1972. A plan of the terminal for 1972 shows the platform area to now be converted to two platforms on an island basis, incoming and outgoing trains using only No. 1, with No. 2 as a siding stop blocked at the east end, access being via a connection from/to the No. 1 platform line.

The horse landing platform on the south side of the sidings became a Motorail Terminal between 1973 and 1976. Following the abandonment of freight sundries in 1972 and full load traffic in single wagons in 1976, all the sidings were removed by 1981/2 when the single running line was slewed to the extreme south side of the yard, leaving facilities only for the few unit passenger trains involved. The illustrations will hopefully show readers how the works developed as the years progressed from 1906 to beyond the millennium.

The final touches are being applied to the new station prior to opening in 1906 for traffic to and from southern Ireland.
(Lens of Sutton)

An official photo of a Paddington to Fishguard Harbour formation with Old Oak Common engine 175. (Author's Collection)

In business…the freight sidings for in and out traffic with two steamers in the bay. The wagons nearest the camera are cattle wagons which have been limed ready for a new supply of cattle to be loaded. Cattle traffic was mainly for Smithfield market in London where an unpleasant fate awaited the new arrivals. (Lens of Sutton)

188 • CARMARTHEN TO FISHGUARD HARBOUR

An Atbara 4-4-0 between Fishguard Harbour and Goodwick with an Irish Mail service for Paddington. (P.Q. Treloar Collection)

A view of the port in November 1906. (Author's Collection)

CARMARTHEN TO FISHGUARD HARBOUR • 189

An Irish Mail steamer arriving at Fishguard in the early years of the port. (Author's Collection)

The sidings at the east end of the complex in the early years of the port. The limed cattle wagons would convey cattle from Ireland bound for Smithfield market and would be a regular sight at the port until the early 1960s. (Author's Collection)

190 • CARMARTHEN TO FISHGUARD HARBOUR

An aerial view of the port from the east end. (Author's Collection)

Fishguard Harbour as operating in the 1920s, with the huge cattle pens dominant, accessed by underground passage from the quay. (Lens of Sutton)

Another view of the station complex from the west end, with two steamers in the Bay. (Lens of Sutton)

The station complex seen from the west end with platforms and transit sheds. (Lens of Sutton)

192 • CARMARTHEN TO FISHGUARD HARBOUR

The east end of No. 2 Platform with freight wagons berthed alongside the platform. (Lens of Sutton)

The east end of the outside platform with passenger stock in the station sidings. (Lens of Sutton)

CARMARTHEN TO FISHGUARD HARBOUR • 193

The east end of the open platform showing the level crossing and a steamer berthed. (Lens of Sutton)

A view out over the harbour on 10 May 1962 showing the sidings still quite full of vanfits and container traffic, with a 2 coach service to Clarbeston Road departing with a Goodwick pannier and the *St David* in the harbour. (Colour Rail)

Two views of the first and later *St Patrick* steamers used from Rosslare to Fishguard.

CARMARTHEN TO FISHGUARD HARBOUR • 195

The *St David* in the 1920s. (P.Q. Treloar Collection)

The *Great Western* at her berth.

An HST connecting service at the outside platform with the *St Brendan* ferry berthed.

The later Stena ferry with rail tracks showing signs of lack of use.

CARMARTHEN TO FISHGUARD HARBOUR • 197

The approaches to Fishguard Harbour from the overbridge at Fishguard & Goodwick station in c1950. (Roger Carpenter)

The outside platform now used for arriving and departing services, as seen in 1955. (R.K. Blencowe Collection)

The 4.10pm to Clarbeston Road awaits departure with 8739 on 22 May 1958. (N.C. Simmons/Hugh Davies)

From an incoming train from Clarbeston Road, the west end of the sidings are recorded with 4644 on shunting duty, empty parcel vans and some freight. A steamer is berthed on its turnround. (P.J. Garland/Roger Carpenter)

Fishguard Harbour Station signal box on 22 May 1963. (P.J. Garland/Roger Carpenter)

A view of the track layout looking west towards the signal box on 22 May 1963. There are container flats in the Up siding and a vessel for Ireland berthed at the quay. Note the trailing connection from the Up to Down main line and the connection from the Up main into the Down main and Up/Down loop. (P.J. Garland/Roger Carpenter)

Goods and freight traffic handled at the undercover platform area on 13 July 1962. (Alan Wild)

Goodwick pannier 9666 marshalling two wagons of cattle for onward transit, probably to London on 27 May 1961. Great care was afforded livestock to ensure they were fed and watered as necessary, especially if they had endured a rough crossing of the Irish Sea. (Alan Wild)

5716 shunting the sidings between the Harbour and Goodwick. (Nigel Wassell Collection)

Container traffic was abundant with 9677 shunting wagons on 6 July 1960. (Colour Rail)

A view on 2 September 1958 from the access road to the Harbour station with the ferry boat *St David* berthed at the quay and Goodwick pannier No. 5713 shunting in the sidings. (Kidderminster Railway Museum)

Carmarthen based 4134 with the 11.45am service to Carmarthen on 2 September 1958. (Kidderminster Railway Museum)

One of the early replacements for the 517 Class auto engines for the Clarbeston Road service was No. 4852 seen here at Bay platform 2 on 25 July 1936. (F.K. Davies)

The last steam passenger train to work to Fishguard Harbour was a joint RCTS/SLS special on 26 September 1965 when Severn Tunnel Junction's Grange No. 6859 *Yiewsley Grange* (with name removed) worked a special from Swansea, seen here ready to return from the main platform, with a diesel shunter marshalling wagons in the siding. (S.B. Lee/Colour Rail)

In this 19 September 1970 shot approaching Goodwick station showing Brush Type 4 D1919 on a train to Swansea overtaking a Hymek on a freight to Margam, we get a last view of the old layout before a new road was built into the terminal and the rail access reduced to a single line. (Garth Tilt)

The new layout as seen on 3 October 1972 with two nests of sidings retained alongside the terminal but the main line to Goodwick and beyond reduced to a single line. (Garth Tilt)

On the same day, 1,750 HP D6884 leaves the Harbour sidings with 7C88 which, if the reporting number is correct, is probably a freight to Margam. Note the Fishguard Bay Hotel on the top left. (Garth Tilt)

A scene at Fishguard Harbour on 25 August 1977.
(R.F. Roberts/SLS)

33020 stands at the Harbour platform with the service from Swansea which will return at 14.38 on 27 September 1982.
(Peter Jones)

33020 waits to leave Fishguard Harbour with the 14.38 to Swansea on 27 September 1982.
(Peter Jones)

Two views of Fishguard Harbour on 17 August 1987 with the 14.10 HST to Paddington at the platform. (Jeff Stone)

Fishguard Harbour on 17 August 1987 with the Stena Ferry to Ireland at the quay. (Jeff Stone)

Fishguard & Rosslare Railways & Harbours Great Western Trespass Notices.

A view of the harbour on 5 July 1967 with the *St David* at the quay and the Marine Stores on the right with the shell harbour within the main harbour.
(Kidderminster Railway Museum)

The four coach 13.35 Fishguard Harbour to Cardiff Central leaves the port station behind 37408, the single line running along the area that used to be the freight sidings. The traffic is now mostly by road as can be seen in this 22 July 2003 scene. (Stuart Warr)

On the last stage of its journey from Cardiff, 37408 runs down the single line from Goodwick station to the Harbour with the 10.47 service from Cardiff Central on 22 July 2003. (Stuart Warr)

The first Class 175 unit to visit Fishguard was on 19 August 2006 when unit 175103 worked the service from Cardiff seen here on the 13.35 return. (Stuart Warr)

CARMARTHEN TO FISHGUARD HARBOUR • 209

The return Fishguard Centenary Special departs from the Harbour station at 16.20 to return to Tyseley with preserved Castle 5051 *Earl Bathurst*, a regular Landore based engine seen at Fishguard in steam days, in charge.
(Peter Jones)

The return Fishguard Centenary Special to Tyseley with assembled crowds, standing at the platform for its 16.20 departure on 19 August 2006.
(Peter Jones)

50049 *Defiance* with the stock of the Centenary Special to be worked back to Tyseley by Castle 5051 *Earl Bathurst* on 19 August 2006. (Peter Jones)

The 14.18 service to Swansea prepares to leave with unit 150259 on 6 June 2010. (Stuart Warr)

The Northern Belle Christmas Lunchtime Experience 12.05 Cardiff Central to Fishguard Harbour with 47832 *Solway Princess* prepares for the return journey on 7 December 2011. (Stuart Warr)

Prior to Christmas 2011, the Northern Belle Christmas Lunch-Time Experience ran to Fishguard Harbour behind Class 47 47832 *Solway Princess*, seen leaving the Harbour station as the 15.00 service to Cardiff Central on 7 December. (Stuart Warr)

APPENDIX

TRAIN SERVICES AT WHITLAND SUMMER 1957

Down Trains   Class C services in RED

AM.	Days	From	To
12.25 pass	MX	6.55pm Paddington	Fishguard Hbr.
12.40 pass	SO	7.5pm FO Paddington	Fishguard Hbr
1.07 – 1.30	SO	2.02pm Old Oak Common	Neyland Fish Empties
1.37 arr.	Sun	4.25pm SO West Ealing	Whitland
4.12-4.17	MX	6.15pm Yeovil	Neyland Parcels
04.16 arr.	MO	7.45pm Kensington	Whitland Milk Empties
4-22-4.26	SO	9.57pm Birmingham	Fishguard
4.36-4.54	MX	8.55pm Paddington	Neyland
5.02 pass	Sun	10.55pm SO Paddington	Fishguard
5.22-6.10	M-S	6.50pm Swindon	Neyland Parcels
		11pm Sun Cdf	Neyland Parcels
5.42-5.50	M-S	1.05am Bristol	Neyland
		9.25pm Sun Paddington	Neyland
6.00 dep.	M-S		Pembroke Dock.
6.20 dep.	M-S		Cardigan
6.37 arr.	MX	7.25pm Wood Lane	Whitland Milk Empties
8.22-8.23	M-S	7.15am Llanelly	Milford Haven
8.50am	MO Q	1.08am Marston	Whitland Milk Empties
9.33-9.38	M-S	8.00 Swansea	Neyland
9.46 dep.	M-S		Pembroke Dock
10.10-10.16	M-S dated	9.15 Llanelly	Pembroke Dock
1033.-10.40	M-S	6.20 Newport	Neyland
10.45 dep	M-S		Pembroke Dock
11.15-11.20	M-S	5.50 Bristol	Pembroke Dock
11.35 dep	M-S		Cardigan
PM.			
1.27-1.32	SO	6.35 Taunton	Neyland
1.39-1.43	SX	1.10 Carmarthen	Neyland
1.54-2.0	SO	9.12 Cardiff	Neyland Parcels
2.11-2.23	SX	7.55 Pdn	Pembroke Dock
2.25 arr	M-S	1.55 Carm LE for	3.50 Whit-Kensington Milk
2.24-2.30	SO	8.40 Paddington	Pembroke Dock
2.53-3.05	SX	8.55 Paddington	Pembroke Dock
2.59-3.07	SO	8.55 Paddington	Pembroke Dock

3.05 dep	SX		Neyland
3.10 dep	SO		Neyland
3.10-3-30	SX	9.12 Cardiff	Neyland Parcels
3.14-3.22	SO	9.10 Birmingham (SH)	Pembroke Dock
3.51-3.54	SO	9.55 Pdn	Neyland
4.00 dep	M-S		Cardigan
4.09-4.15	SX	10.55 Paddington	Pembroke Dock
4.20 dep	SX		Neyland
4.25 arr	M-S	3.50 LE ex-Carm for	5.15 Whit-Kens Milk
4.47-4.53	SO	10.55 Paddington	Pembroke Dock
4.55 dep	SO		Neyland
5.2-5.24	SO	12.30 Shrewsbury	Pembroke Dock
5.26-5.31	SO	11.35 Paddington	Pembroke Dock
5.46-5.54	SX	11.55 Paddington	Pembroke Dock
6.00 dep	M-S		Milford Haven
6.07-6.15	SO	11.55 Paddington	Pembroke Dock
6.15 dep	SX		Cardigan
6.20 dep	SO		Milford Haven
6.25 dep	SO		Cardigan
7.55 arr	M-S	7.15 Carm. LE to work	8.30pm Whit-Kens Milk
8.03 pass	SO	2.55 Paddington	Fishguard
8.28-8.36	SX	1.55 Paddington	Pembroke Dock
8.34-8.42	SO	1.55 Paddington	Pembroke Dock
8.42 dep	SX		Neyland
8.47 dep	SO		Neyland
9.00 pass	SX	4.02 Weston	Fishguard
9.11 pass	M-S	3.45 Paddington	Fishguard
9.49-9.51	M-S	3.55 Paddington	Fishguard
9.55 dep	M-S		Pembroke Dock
10.32 arr	SX	10.35 Kensington	Whitland Milk Empties
11.8-1123	SX	12.45 Old Oak Common	Neyland Fish Empties

Up Trains

AM.	Days	From	To
4.21 pass	SO	3.35 Fishguard	Paddington
4.43 pass	MX	3.55 Fishguard	Paddington
5.14 pass	MX	4.25 Fishguard	Paddington
5.41 pass	MX	4.55 Fishguard	Paddington
7.00 dep	MX	Whitland	Carm off Kens. Milk Etys.
8.34 arr	M-S	6.50 Cardigan	
8.43 arr	SX	7.30 Pembroke Dock	
8.43-8.50	SO	7.30 Pembroke Dock	Paddington

AM.	Days	From	To
8.56-9.03	M-S	8.00 Neyland	Paddington
9.44-9.50	SO	8.30 Pembroke Dock	Birmingham (SH)
9.47-9.57	M-S	8.48 Fishguard	Paddington Parcels
10.45-10.51	SO	9.30 Pembroke Dock	Shrewsbury
11.23-11.25	M-S	10.35 Neyland	Carmarthen
11.40 arr	M-S	10.00 Cardigan	
11.47 arr	SX	10.20 Pem.Dk.	
11.47-11.53	SO	10.20 Pembroke Dock	Paddington
11.57-12.04	M-S	11.10 Milford Haven	Paddington
PM.			
12.39-12.41	M-S	11.45 Fishguard	Carmarthen
12.45 arr	M-S	11.25 Pem.Dk.	
12.53-1.00	M-S	12.05 Milford Haven	Paddington
1.19-1.24	SO	12.05 Pembroke Dock	Paddington
2.21-2.26	M-S	1.05 Pembroke Dock	Paddington
2.45 arr	SX	1.30 Pembroke Dock	
2.53 pass	FO Q	2.5 Milford Haven	Cardiff Fish
2.57 arr	SO	1.40 Pembroke Dock	
3.50 dep	M-S		Kensington Milk
4.08 pass	M-S	3.20 Milford Haven	Carmarthen Fish
4.40 pass	M-S	3.50 Milford Haven	Severn Tunnel Jct. Fish
5.15 dep	M-S Q		Kensington Milk
5.17 arr	SX	3.50 Pembroke Dock	
5.22 arr	SO	3.55 Pembroke Dock	
5.24-5.29	M-S	4.25 Neyland	Cardiff
6.05 pass	SO	5.15 Fishguard	Paddington Dated
6.08 pass Q	M-S	5.20 Milford Haven	Paddington Fish
6.28-6.43	M-S	4.35 Neyland	Paddington Parcels
7.05 arr	M-S	6.10 Neyland	
7.18-7.24	M-S	5.55 Pembroke Dock	Llanelly
7.28 arr	M-S	5.45 Cardigan	
7.32-7.43	M-S	6.15 Pembroke Dock	Swansea
7.48-7.55	M-S	6.50 Neyland	Paddington
8.30 dep	M-S		Kensington Milk
9.22 arr	M-S	8.00 Pembroke Dock	
9.27-9.45	M-S	7.50 Neyland	Cardiff Parcels
11.10 pass	SO	10.20 Fishguard	Swansea ECS

Q = Runs when Required